Learning to Be an Associate Provost

Learning to Be an Associate Provost

A Playbook to Understanding the Role to Developing Collegial Relationships

Janet Tareilo

ROWMAN & LITTLEFIELD
Lanham • Boulder • New York • London

Published by Rowman & Littlefield
An imprint of The Rowman & Littlefield Publishing Group, Inc.
4501 Forbes Boulevard, Suite 200, Lanham, Maryland 20706
www.rowman.com

86 –90 Paul Street, London EC2A 4NE

British Library Cataloguing in Publication Information Available

Library of Congress Cataloging-in-Publication Data

Names: Tareilo, Janet, author.
Title: Learning to be an associate provost : a playbook to understanding
   the role to developing collegial relationships / Janet Tareilo.
Description: Lanham, Maryland : Rowman & Littlefield, 2023. | Includes
   bibliographical references. | Summary: "Through the many chapters of
   this book, lived experiences will provide a "real world" look at the
   position of the associate provost"-- Provided by publisher.
Identifiers: LCCN 2023015628 (print) | LCCN 2023015629 (ebook) | ISBN
   9781475868326 (cloth) | ISBN 9781475868333 (paperback) | ISBN
   9781475868340 (ebook)
Subjects: LCSH: College administrators--United States--Handbooks, manuals,
   etc. | College administrators--Professional relationships--United
   States--Handbooks, manuals, etc. | Universities and colleges--United
   States--Administration--Handbooks, manuals, etc.
Classification: LCC LB2341 .T26 2023 (print) | LCC LB2341 (ebook) | DDC
   378.1/11--dc23/eng/20230505
LC record available at https://lccn.loc.gov/2023015628
LC ebook record available at https://lccn.loc.gov/2023015629

Contents

Foreword

While I was growing up in rural Texas, the annual trip to the state fair in Dallas (a school-sponsored trip, by the way) was a really big deal. The sights, sounds, and experiences that awaited us on that trip each year were unique, something we really had never been part of before. It was fun, exciting, and different. So, when I saw the title of this book comparing the role of associate provost to a state fair, I admit to being a bit skeptical. Fun, games, and surprises? I wasn't quite sure. And, after much thought and reflection, I realize this might just be the greatest metaphor ever.

The role of associate provost is fun, exciting, and different from any previous role an academic may have had . . . just as I described the state fair experience I had while growing up. Becoming an associate provost presents challenges that a faculty member likely never had to face or even consider. And, frankly, we don't do enough to prepare people for this critically important role.

We in academia do very little to actually prepare leaders for the challenges that await them. The skills and accomplishments that make someone a highly successful faculty member, most often related to excellence in research, teaching, and service, are only tangentially related to the skills needed to be a successful leader.

The typical faculty member has limited, if any, direct responsibility for formally evaluating staff or faculty and even less responsibility for working with individuals who are having performance issues or who may be behaving badly. Faculty also have almost no responsibility for budget or fiscal decision-making. They have almost no expectation of engaging with policy, especially at the state or federal level; nor are they typically expected to interact in any way with policymakers. Yet, successfully working with people (especially difficult people!), policies, and budgets is among the most critical functions of academic leaders at almost any institution.

We offer little to no preparation for this type of role and yet somehow expect people to transition seamlessly and effectively from faculty to academic leader. We owe our current and future leaders more than that, more than a few tickets or a bus ride to the fair with no map, no preparation, no guidance.

What is the role of associate provost, anyway? The role itself is ill-defined, particularly because it varies by institution and is largely dependent on context. Perhaps your focus as associate provost will be on ways to increase and maximize student success, with an emphasis on first-generation students or students from historically disadvantaged backgrounds. Or perhaps your role will be dedicated to increasing faculty success, with responsibility for evaluation, research support, or teaching effectiveness.

Even more likely, your role will include a number of things that fall under the "other duties as assigned" category, meaning that your menu of responsibility will include a variety of important and diverse (and perhaps, at times, seemingly unrelated) endeavors, such as policy development, accreditation reporting, or data analytics.

Undoubtedly, whatever the role involves, it will include working with a multitude of different people, managing a large number of interests and perspectives, and frequently reflecting on how to prioritize competing responsibilities and tasks. In fact, you can just about be guaranteed to feel like your job is almost always about juggling and often like wandering in a house of mirrors . . . a lot like visiting the state fair!

The days of an associate provost are most always exciting, and no two days are ever the same. And, as at the state fair, there will be things you enjoy and a few things you do not. The opportunities will be fun, sometimes risky, often exhausting, and almost always rewarding.

This book offers practical advice for how to navigate the adventure of being an associate provost, in a style that is fun, relatable, and entertaining. Academic leadership is hard work, and providing tools for navigating this important position is important as we build the next generation of college and university leaders. Our students deserve leaders who are prepared, dedicated, and excited about the opportunity to impact higher education in meaningful ways.

In fact, the future of higher education depends on this type of impactful leader. May we all, then, approach academic leadership with as much excitement—and joy—as a day at the fair and embrace the fun, games, and surprises that lie ahead?

Dr. Stacey Edmonson Victor
Dean, College of Education
Sam Houston State University

Preface

If a person wants to be good, really good, at something, he or she will find books on the subject, will meet and talk with people who have had relevant experiences, or will spend hours in a library, doing research on the subject.

What are you supposed to do when there are very few books on the subject, when people who have had pertinent experiences are not available, and libraries lack information about the subject?

Simple. You write a book about your own lived experiences. You join a group of administrators that hold your same position, and you make sure the library gets a copy of the book you write.

When I was named as the associate provost for our university, I had an inkling, a very small inkling, of what was coming my way. I had been an elementary-school principal for sixteen years, a program director, and an associate dean for two years. I had some ideas about leadership and how to build positive relationships.

As an elementary-school principal, I had led a school through a tornado, lived through a bomb threat, been nudged by a car during afternoon student pick-up duty, and had parents arrested when they caused dangerous situations on the campus.

Being an elementary school principal and being an associate dean provided some basic skills and learned abilities. But, when I was named the associate provost, there was very little time to learn everything else I needed to know. Additionally, the provosts had heavy workloads and very little time to train me in the ways of higher education. I had to be learn independently how to be an associate provost.

Even with all of these abilities in my bag of tricks, I was still unprepared for many of the tasks that were assigned to me and for what was expected of me during my tenure as an associate provost. No guidelines were provided, and even the job description was vague at best.

I thought that, to help me learn about what was needed to be successful in the position, somewhere there had to be a user's manual or a YouTube video on how to be an associate provost and survive the role. However, I found nothing, nada, not a thing.

So, I wrote a book. That's right: Little old me, who had served in the role of an associate provost for only a few short years, I wrote a book filled with real lived experiences. I included stories about relationships and connections that I developed and fostered and many accounts of the role I played in helping students that came to my door. Of course, I also included some suggestions of what not to do while serving as an administrator in higher education.

I had a purpose for writing this book. When I began my role as the new associate provost, I wanted to be successful in the position. Vain, maybe, but I also didn't want to make any mistakes that would in any way bring harm to my institution or its people.

If I could write down a few ideas, suggestions, or recommendations that I had learned along my journey as a newly appointed associate provost, maybe another person in this same situation could "hit the ground running," so to speak.

Having competent and well-informed leaders is essential to the success of any organization. An associate provost holds a leadership position in an institution of higher education. Decisions that are made while serving in that role could and will impact the entire academic community. Having a user's manual, such as this book, might come in handy to those serving in this leadership role.

Every chapter focuses on what I learned and on the people who entered my life while I served in the position of associate provost. Don't get me wrong. I made some mistakes; however, I made them only once. Sure, on occasion, I said a few things that I shouldn't have been said at that particular time. You guessed it: I said those things only once.

I would love to watch your face as you read some of the stories and suggestions in this book and react to what I said or did. Perhaps you will think to yourself, "She did what? She said what?" Perhaps some of the suggestions I provide will make you say, "Oh, I wouldn't have ever thought of doing that."

Reading this book as an aspiring associate provost or even as an associate provost who has served for many years will hopefully ignite or reignite in you the need to serve, the purpose to help students achieve academic goals, and the desire to be a leader of an institution of higher education that moves the academic community forward.

This book might not be the be-all and end-all resource for learning how to be a successful associate provost, and is it a little vain? You betcha. But I think it's a pretty good start.

Acknowledgment

Learning something new always takes time and some trial and error. There will be a couple of learning curves along the way. That's exactly what happened when I began my career as an associate provost at an institution of higher education.

As a visual learner, I don't like to read instructions. Just show me how to do something, and I can generally do what is needed. Don't tell me how to find something on a map. Just show me. However, there are no maps or visual clues to help guide novice associate provosts in learning the ropes and responsibilities of the position.

Most positions I have held had a probationary period, a time for learning. When I became a concession-stand worker and poured beer, I had to learn how to tip a cup exactly right to reduce the amount of suds. I also had to learn how much oil to add to a popcorn machine to get the right buttery taste.

Were there times, when I first started working in concession stands, that I burned some popcorn? Of course. Were there times when I poured beer into a cup and there were too many suds? Yes, indeed. I was learning. When I finished working in concession stands forty years later (part-time, here and there), I had beer pouring and popcorn making down to an art.

When I was named as the new associate provost for my university, I definitely faced a learning curve. I kept thinking of some old sayings that might best describe my feelings at this time:

- Trial by fire,
- Leap and a net will appear (John Burroughs), and
- Sink or swim—it's your choice

As with any job I ever have undertaken, I jumped in with both feet, always hoping for the best. After three years of serving in the role of associate provost, I had learned what I needed to learn and was headed towards retirement. Until . . .

Until a colleague of mine, Dr. Gina Anderson, called to let me know she was applying for the position of associate provost at her university. She wanted to know if I could give her some insight into the world of the position. About an hour into our conversation, she mentioned I should write a book about my life as an associate provost.

Being retired and with some time on my hands, I thought that was a good idea. This thought was affirmed when I started researching information on the position of associate provost and found very few resources on how to be successful—much less on what to do—in the position.

So, here's the book that will hopefully tell the story of a novice associate provost, some lessons she learned and some that should be forgotten, as well as memories of wonderful times serving as an administrator for a university.

As always, I could not have written one word without the encouragement of my husband, Kirk, and my daughters, Amanda and Jenny. They have always been and will always be at the center of everything I do. They and many others (adopted family members and my grandchildren, Ezra and Eisley) are proof that a heart can actually walk outside the human body.

However, others must also be recognized in this writing effort. These are the people that I worked with and for, the students who came to me for help and guidance, and those who let me follow them as I learned the skills of being a leader in higher education.

To all of the above and many others, you have my gratitude and appreciation for all the lessons I learned.

Introduction

While this book was still just an idea, I kept searching for the right analogy to illustrate what it is like to be a newly appointed associate provost.

The subtitle of the book uses the word "playbook." So, I thought about using "Getting to Know Special Teams" or "Hurry to the Hurdle" as possible titles for some of the chapters. Those titles didn't sound right or really convey the entire concept I was looking for. Then I toyed with the concept of learning and thought of possible titles for chapters, such as "Learning the Ropes" or "Learning is for Everyone." Those titles didn't sound right either.

After a few days of in-depth thinking, I finally came up with the one concept that could actually help describe what life is like as a novice associate provost: a day at the fair. A fair, especially the State Fair of Texas, has something for everyone.

There are slow and scary rides, much like the days I spent working as an administrator in higher education. Choosing from the many food options at a fair parallels how an associate provost must make many decisions. A visit to a fair was the perfect way to tell the story of how a newly assigned associate provost learned how to live and work in the role.

This memoir of sorts began with a simple suggestion from a friend and turned out to be a very cathartic experience. Reliving many of the experiences that I had as a new associate provost reminded me of how much I really loved serving in the position as well as meeting and working with amazing people while I served.

Let's say you are attending a conference focused on leadership in higher education and you happen to pass by the Author's Corner. There, in a very prominent display, a new book grabs your attention: *Learning to Be an Associate Provost: A Playbook to Understanding the Role to Developing Collegial Relationships*. Because you have always wanted to be a leader in the world of academia, you pick up the book and start flipping through the first few pages. The chapter titles in the Table of Contents, such as "Planning a Day at the Fair" and "Fried Butter and More," and your inquisitive nature get the best of you.

What is this book going to be about? What do the words "associate provost," "playbook," and "fair" have in common? And, more importantly, how is this book going to help with acquiring a position as an associate provost?

Let me provide some clarity.

This book is not about how to acquire the position. This book, every word in every chapter, relates to how to be successful while in the position and how to build and maintain needed relationships. Most importantly, this book makes suggestions about how to be an effective associate provost for the institution's academic community. This book addresses those who are serving in the position, including those who might need to be reminded why they serve.

Each chapter begins with a description of some part or place on the grounds of the State Fair of Texas, which is located in Dallas, Texas. As you continue reading, correlations are made between a day at the fair and the job, tasks, and responsibilities of an associate provost. You will notice that this book is organized by various academic elements, focuses on actions that associate provosts should take and some that they should not take, and provides pieces of advice that helped me.

With a little humor, mindful storytelling, and plausible suggestions and recommendations, the experiences of a newly appointed associate provost are told in order to bring a realistic understanding of the position to those who are serving as associate provosts.

The book you are reading recounts my story, my own experiences. Your story is yet to be told. It is my hope that from reading this memoir you may gain some meaningful insight into the important and necessary role of an associate provost and that maybe, just maybe, something you read in one of the chapters leads to your success, the building of meaningful academic relationships, and a balance in your life-work world.

Chapter 1

Going to the Fair (Accepting the Position of Associate Provost)

Every September in Dallas, Texas, the State Fair of Texas comes to town and stays for twenty-four days. According to readers.com, the State Fair of Texas is the largest fair in the United States, with almost 2.25 million visitors per year. During those twenty-four days, a person can take part in different festivities offered by the park, visit a variety of exhibits, and select from an amazing number of food choices.

The fair is a magical place where every visitor's experience is unique. There are exhibits, from the Automobile Building, which holds every new truck and car imaginable, to the petting zoo, where baby animals of all kinds are just waiting to be fed little alfalfa pellets, to explore. And the food! The food is an event in itself.

Of course, there is the Midway, where games and rides are just waiting for the next willing customer. The sounds emanating from the rides range from joyous laughter to screams of fear. Barkers stand at each game site enticing you to play their games of chance. You can throw basketballs, toss rings on tops of empty two-liter bottles, or shoot water pistols into the mouths of racing ducks just to win some prize—usually a stuffed animal.

The State Fair of Texas is definitely the place to be when September rolls around. Tickets allow you to play any game, ride any ride, and buy any kind of food you want. A map given to you when you enter the front gates helps guide you around the fairgrounds so you don't miss one special thing.

THE BEGINNING

For anyone interested in entering the field of higher education, there is definitely a game plan in place. There is a starting point, becoming an assistant professor in a particular college, and a possible ending point, becoming an

1

administrator there. Not every professor seeks to become an administrator; some do not want to take on that particular level of responsibility, and some are not called to serve at that level.

The track that you have used to assume the role of an associate provost could have taken several paths. Maybe you have previously served as an assistant or associate professor. If you are an internal candidate for the position, your name might already be known across the community. Or, if you are an external candidate for the position, your experience might already be that of an associate provost and you are making a lateral move.

Whichever the trajectory your academic leadership journey has taken, taking on the role of an associate provost centers on dedication and a continued desire to serve an academic community. Those serving as associate provosts should be hardworking, committed to the institution, and devoted to excellence in teaching. The path to a future leadership position is in the works.

Taking on any leadership role in higher education, especially that of associate provost, is most assuredly not for the faint of heart. On many campuses, an associate provost is in line to lead the university when the president, the vice presidents, and the provost are off campus or otherwise unavailable. This means that you, in the role of an associate provost, might very well be responsible for the campus for that time. Your leadership abilities will be called into service.

Accordingly, your role as an associate provost may include the "short-term power" of making university decisions, of addressing faculty problems, or of greeting a gathering of campus visitors. You must be prepared and readied to take on extra duties of university leadership when other administrators are off campus or otherwise unavailable.

You might be thinking to yourself that your resume, on paper, shows the history of your leadership experiences and your ability to serve in the role of associate provost. You feel confident that your capacity for problem-solving and discernment have been recognized. What you don't know is how to be an associate provost. This level of leadership requires your skills to be on steroids, so to speak.

To understand your role better, begin with the job description. When you applied for the position, you were given a job description that listed primary and secondary duties. Those duties were written somewhat vaguely to leave the interpretation of the responsibility open, open especially to the provost's interpretation. The one duty that should grab your attention is the one that states, "all other duties as assigned."

Even after reading the job duties of an associate provost, you decided that you want to pursue becoming an associate provost. You applied for an open associate provost position, went through the interview process, and, lo and behold, you have been selected to be the new associate provost. After the celebratory high fives and the well wishes from friends and faculty, you are faced with a very real thought. How do you become an associate provost? You have the position, you have the leadership abilities, and you are anxious to serve. Now, where do you start learning the ropes of the position, and, what is the right starting point? At the very beginning, of course. Before you fill out all the paperwork, before you move into a new office, and even before you buy that new sofa (thinking about your new salary), you must know a few basics:

- You and the provost should be seen as a team working in tandem to serve the academic community at the university. Try your best to create a positive working relationship with the provost as early as possible.
- Unless you develop an early life-work balance (this will be discussed later), your time now belongs to the institution. Faculty members have a number of required hours they must be in their offices or on the campus. Administrators, including associate provosts, do not. You are always on duty.
- No personal situation enters into your world as an associate provost. Does that mean you can't go to the dentist or take a few days off to visit family? Of course not. If you need a couple of days to address personal situations, take them. You need to be 100-percent present every day that you are not on personal leave.
- Staff and faculty across the institution depend on you being 100-percent present and giving 100 percent of your effort. Try your best to give them as many 100-percent days as you can.
- Keep a spare set of "professional" clothes in your office just in case you are called upon to serve as a representative for your institution. Just do it. You'll know why if you ever have to use it.

There are certainly more basics that you should be aware of, and the chapters in this book will hopefully give you the insight to be a success in your new role.

YOUR HOME AWAY FROM HOME

Because you will be spending many waking hours at the university, you need to have a place that gives you a sense of peace as well as an organized work space in order to accomplish the many tasks you will be assigned. Your office should reflect your role as a university administrator and be comfortable enough that it's a place where you want to work.

The climate in your office sends a message to all who enter. If you are not a feng shui master or a Martha Stewart follower, your office space needs to be a comfortable space for others as well as for you. This space also needs to reflect the position you hold. Evidence of degrees and awards that you have earned needs to line your walls. Such a display gives visitors to your office a sense of confidence in your abilities and credibility.

This may sound trite. The truth of the matter is that the decor you choose for your office space actually speaks to your role as an associate provost. For instance, if you choose to put your collection of Hello Kitty decorations around your office, a visitor or even the provost might consider this a little elementary and may begin to wonder about your maturity level or even about your ability to do your job.

Think of your office as a professional place to work as well as a place to relax when the day is done. Having family pictures and personal knickknacks helps to create that sense of peace you will often need. OK, if you have to have something with the Hello Kitty design on it, make it a small reflection piece and put it in a place where only you can see it.

Many universities house all of their administrators in one place, which is actually very advantageous because meetings are frequent and being able to answer questions at a moment's notice is valuable. With that said, administrators from across the university may well visit your office on a daily basis. You want to leave them with the impression that your work area is the work area of a professional.

Regardless of where your office is located, make sure it is well-kept, professional in nature, and a little comfortable, especially for you. The space you claim as your office also has to be a safe and inviting place for people to come to. You want to create an environment that is open and welcoming. Here are a few suggestions for building that kind of professional working space:

- If space is sufficient, put a table in your office. Use this table for meetings that center around easy conversations. If you want to let others know you hold a position of authority, stay at your desk. Sometimes you might actually want to move a meeting to a conference room away from your office space.
- Avoid having chairs in front of your desk. This gives the impression that people should stay and get comfy. Use the chairs from the extra table in your office as chairs for your desk meetings, and then move them back to their original places.
- Depending on the type of meeting you are having, the door may need to be closed. Closing the door keeps the conversation confidential and gives your visitor the impression that he or she can speak openly to you.

For some meetings, the difficult ones, the door may need to stay open to provide a witness for the conversation that is taking place.

- If you have some kind of collection in your office, keep the collection away from your meeting area. Some people put their collections of bobblehead figures or unicorns all over their offices. Having a bobble-head figure or a collection of Hot Wheel cars might bring you a sense of peace. If that is the case, put the collection somewhere that you can see it but that will not interfere with you being seen as a professional.
- Place a memo board outside of your office. Messages on the board let others know where you are and when you might return to your office. These messages could be "Gone to lunch," "Be back soon," or "Come on in." Providing such messages allows others to know when you will be back in the office and protects your time and theirs.

Establishing your office space seems like a very small cog in the wheel of all your responsibilities as an associate provost; yet it is important. Make your office space your own, make it comfortable as well as professional, and design it for your success in the role. Whether you have the decorating skills of Martha Stewart or Atilla the Hun, setting up your own space probably won't be the hardest thing you face in your role.

INTRODUCTIONS

You have been named as one of the associate provosts for your institution. Your new name badge, showing your name and that new position, is being created. You have your new office, and you can even park in the special spaces reserved for university administrators. During a welcome back meeting, your name has been mentioned as the newly appointed associate provost. The academic community has been informed, and, the minute that happens, you are on immediate duty to the university.

The president, the provost, and the vice presidents know who you are. While having name recognition is very beneficial (well, most of the time), how are you going to let the staff and faculty around the campus know that you are the newly appointed associate provost? What actions can you take to let the others know of your commitment to the university and them? Don't assume that the people of the institution know what you can do just because they know your name.

The role of the associate provost cannot be confined to one department or one college. This role encompasses every academic department, all staff and faculty members in various departments, and every "side of the house," with the "house" being the institution. The "other side of the house" refers to the university department's side of the institution. The academic side of the house is where you and the provost will address any and all academic situations that arise. Knowing who serves on each side of the house is of great importance to you and your success.

Many of those who work outside the academic realm know very little about what an associate provost actually does for a university. These staff members work in such areas as food services, maintenance and grounds, policing, parking, and housing. Sometimes their work behind the scenes tends to be forgotten. While your involvement in the activities that take place on the other side of the house might not take place on a day-to-day basis, you should recognize such staff members for their services and their abilities.

If you have previously served in a leadership position, hopefully you already know that all people, regardless of their position, should be respected and treated with dignity. There is an old adage in leadership that states if you take care of your people, they will take care of you. Taking care of all people, regardless of the position they hold, is nonnegotiable when working in university administration.

As you talk to and work with staff members and academics around the university, do not forget to introduce yourself to those who work behind the scenes. Very simply put, make a point of knowing those who serve in the areas mentioned above. They are vital to the success of the institution as well as to your success. If you are a people person, this task will be an easy one.

But let's say you are not that much of a people person. How should you proceed in the quest to learn about all the people who make up the academic community? Here are a few suggestions that might help as you start to learn about the people you serve.

- When you are named as the newly appointed associate provost, locate the university's organizational chart and make a copy of it. This chart usually names directors of offices and departments, deans, associate deans, and academic coordinators as well as other university employees. This knowledge is vital for you, especially if you are not familiar with the university.
- Once you have the chart, create a plan of action for you to introduce yourself around the campus to the various offices and personnel. This might be a check-off list or a highlighted line through a name. Whatever method you choose, make sure to take the time to meet as many staff and faculty members as possible as soon as you can.
- When you attend a meeting and some of the attendees have positions on the other side of the house, and there is someone you have not previously met, be sure to make your introduction. The introduction should
- serve as an opportunity to meet others and introduce yourself,

- focus on the other person and not on you as the associate provost,
- serve as an opportunity to ask where the other person works and the role he or she plays at the university, and
- give the other person the impression that you stand ready to help him or her if the need ever arises.
- Do your best to earn the respect of others. If you have previously served in a leadership position, you already know the importance of earning someone's respect. Respect can't be bought. It must be earned.

Many of the people in the service side of the house will see your position before they see you as an individual. Learn names quickly. Learn about various positions that are in the departments (director, associate director). Let your conversations revolve around others and their importance, not yours. These suggestions are probably very familiar to you if you have previously served in a leadership position. Now, as you serve in one of the highest positions in academia, don't forget them.

CREATING YOUR OWN PERSONAL BRAND

Regardless of the type of leadership positions you may have previously held, the position of associate provost requires a dual type of leadership. Because of your continual work with faculty, one part of you will still live in the world of academics. And, because you are a member of the administrative team at the university, you will also be required to live in that world.

Providing such dual leadership requires you to work hand in hand with faculty and the provost to support the academic goals of the university. You will be working directly with deans and faculty members who want you to be truly interested in their needs. If they ask you for help or assistance, you must do your best, within the parameters of your position, to fulfill their requests. Your credibility with other academics and in your position as an associate provost is at stake.

In your efforts to bring your own personal brand to the position of an associate provost, your work with others needs to reflect your trustworthiness, dependability, and honesty. One of the most important aspects of building positive relationships with the academics at your institution centers on the support you can give them from within the parameters of your role.

Building positive relationships with the academic community is no different from building such relationships with those who work on the other side of the house. Do you walk around campus telling the groundskeepers that their trees are looking good this year? Do you thank the university police officers when they give out tickets to students who park in your parking spot? Should you pat the cafeteria lady on the back when the mashed potatoes served that day are light and fluffy? You can certainly do this and more. Recognition for a job well done, regardless of whether the person is an academic or a staff member, helps in your efforts to build relationships.

Most of the situations that you will deal with come from the academic side of the house. That is where the authority of your position lies. However, there will be instances when directors and staff members from the other side of the house will need your help. Such individuals might have a family member who needs to meet with an academic advisor and who doesn't know where to start. Maybe a staff member would like to complete his or her own degree and needs some help with financial planning. You can be there to help. Remember, you are new to the position and are trying to do the best job possible for faculty and staff. So, what are some personal characteristics you need when developing your brand as you work with staff members? That's right. You need to be trustworthy, dependable, honest, and supportive.

SINCERITY

"Don't blow smoke up my skirt."
"I've heard that before."
"The last associate provost said she would help, and nothing ever happened."

As you begin working in your position, you might hear one or all of the above statements. These comments focus on missed promises and opportunities to serve the academic community. They reflect on attitudes that were insincere. Don't be surprised if you hear one of these sayings or more. Be prepared to return a comment that shows you are committed to changing a current impression. Your comments should

- be positive;
- avoid blaming others;
- focus on possibilities; and
- offer possible new solutions.

When you start visiting the offices and departments on the organizational chart, have a purpose in mind. Introductions should be made. Asking questions about how the particular office or department works opens lines of communication. Identifying a contact person in the office will come in handy as situations come to your attention.

As mentioned, have a purpose in mind when visiting these offices. Establishing yourself as a sincere person when working with the academics, especially the deans of the colleges, will take some work and effort on your part. Some of the deans will set high expectations for you. They will want to know exactly what you can do for them. Deans are always taking care of their faculty and colleges. They will have the same expectations of you.

There are a few ways you can help yourself to be seen as a sincere and caring associate provost. You can choose to:

- speak about what you know;
- speak the truth;
- use your words wisely;
- listen to what others have to say before you speak; and
- let your words reflect the authority of your position.

Your actions and words, as you build relationships with faculty and staff at your institution, will show your sincerity. You are branding yourself and your abilities with each interaction. You will certainly have the opportunity to become a servant leader as well as a successful associate provost.

GUARDING YOUR WORDS

If your intentions are to be a caring, sincere, and dependable associate provost, you must learn to guard your words. The words you speak have to be grounded in truth and you can't ever let others see how their words have affected you. This is usually the case when you are in meetings with others. Your first instinct might be to say what's on your mind. It will be in your best interest to wait for a better time to react than in a meeting.

Even though you do not speak for the provost, you represent the provost. Even though you have the authority of a campus administrator, the words you use don't necessarily have the support of the provost. Guarding your words means you think about the message you really want to deliver and about whether the recipient understands your intent. Remember, when you speak, you represent the academic community of the institution.

Maybe holding your tongue is not your best trait. Maybe you tend to say the first thing that comes into your mind. Serving in this role requires you to be mindful of the words you use, makes you aware of the audience you are addressing, and hopefully makes you mindful of what your words mean to others. You can learn to guard your words. Following are some pointers in learning this skill.

- Always remember your audience. There are times to use and times not to use educational jargon. Know who you are talking to.
- Have purpose in your words. What message are you really trying to convey?
- When you are in a meeting and someone takes the opportunity to disagree with something you said, be respectful with your response. You can always have a conversation later.
- When you are in a meeting with a faculty member and they don't exactly remember a situation that occurred the same way you do, hear them out. State your side of things and determine where the miscommunication occurred.
- If you are in a meeting with faculty and they become angry, it serves no purpose for you to use angry words in return. Let them have their say and wait for the right time to address the situation. Remember, you can always leave a situation that becomes volatile.
- Use positive affirmations.
- If you make a promise, keep it.
- Be sincere, kind, and considerate.

Your words and how you address situations will certainly reflect on your ability to lead, guide, and build relationships. You might forget what you said, but others will not. You might not remember the way a situation took place; let others have their say. You'll have a chance to respond. Remember, guarding your words doesn't mean you don't get to have an opinion. It does mean you have to be aware of what you are saying.

IMPORTANCE OF CONFIDENTIALITY

"Can you keep a secret?"
"I mean it, you can't tell anyone."
"If I tell you something, you have to keep it to yourself."

In the realm of higher education, confidentiality is not a request, it is a must! As an associate provost, you are privy to many conversations about the workings of the institution, financial matters, hiring practices, and academic decisions. Don't wait to be told something is confidential. Assume everything is confidential.

Keeping confidences might be a little difficult if you were at the institution before becoming the associate provost, especially if you had many friends and acquaintances across the campus. These folks might think that, since you were friends in your past role, you should share information about what happens at the administrative level. Don't share anything. You can always ask the provost what he or she would like you to say if you are asked about a particular situation.

First of all, you don't speak for the provost or the president unless they give you permission to deliver a message or to announce a decision that has been previously made. Friends you have made at the university might sometimes think you are "in the know" and want to hear the "skinny" on university business. As far as you are concerned, you know nothing. You will find an appropriate way to respond.

If you find yourself in a situation where a friend, a faculty member, or a staff member asks what you know about a situation, possibly a situation that involves the university's budget, you certainly want to be respectful, truthful, and sincere, and you want your response to be one that helps grow relationships. Remind these folks

- that you have been in budget meetings and you have limited information on the final decision,
- that the final decision will be made by the president,
- that, whatever decision is made, it will be made in the best interests of the university, and
- that, when the provost or the president allows you to share information, you will.

So that you may be sincere and, at the same time, maintain confidentiality when responding to faculty members, staff members, friends, and acquaintances, always ask the provost what information you can share and with whom you may share it. Let the provost's decision guide your conversation. In this way, the provost knows you will share only what he or she has allowed you to share.

Also, if you have told someone you will get back to him or her with some information, be sure to do just that. Keep your word. These actions will help build your credibility with the provost and others.

SAVING THE BEST FOR LAST

So far, this chapter has shed light on your beginnings as a newly hired associate provost. As you begin your own personal journey as an associate provost, there are a few more pieces of advice for the last part of this chapter.

Unless you are or have been associated with your university in a faculty or academic administrative position (perhaps you served as an associate dean or dean), you may not be well acquainted with the person who holds the position of provost. Sometimes the title of the provost is given to the vice president of academic affairs for the institution. The provost serves as your immediate supervisor, and you, therefore, should learn as much as you can about the provost and you should learn it as fast as you can.

The role of the provost at any institution of higher education is integral to the academic workings of that institution. The provost's actions and accomplishments are essential to the success of the university as a whole. In your service as an associate provost, one of the most important aspects of your job is to provide as much support as you can to the provost. Therefore, it is essential you learn as much as you can about how the provost works and their expectations of you.

Learning how the provost works and their expectations for you may take a little time. So, as you face this particular learning curve, here are a few ideas for your consideration:

- When you are in meetings with the provost, be mindful of how they respond to questions. Are their replies a bit snippy? Do they like to table decisions until further data can be collected and shared? Watch for the way the provost handles decision-making situations.
- During any meeting you have with the provost, take copious notes. There is a specific reason for this. You never know when, whether at a meeting or in a one-on-one meeting with the provost, you will be asked to recall a specific part of a conversation. Devise a way (electronic or written) to keep track of these meeting notes. Your memory and the provost's recall might be a little fuzzy at times, but the notes you take serve as an invaluable source of information.
- Develop a system to remember when a task or action has been assigned to you. You could create a to-do list and reward yourself with a check mark when a task is completed. Or you could write your tasks on Post-It notes and, when a job is done, simply throw the relevant yellow note away. Tasks and responsibilities will be numerous. For your sake and the sake of getting things done, find a system that works best for you.
- Whenever you are given a task by the provost, be sure to ask when the task needs to be completed. Time frames are always of great importance to the workings of the provost's office. If your plate is already full of tasks that have to be completed (and it will be), while talking with the provost, provide possible suggestions for a time for the task to be finished.
- If the provost asks you to look into a certain situation, create a reporting form that has the dates, the situation, the people involved, a summary of the information you were able to find, and possible recommendations. The keyword here is "possible." You can provide suggestions but stay

away from telling the provost what to do. Use this form consistently when reporting back to the provost so the provost becomes acquainted with your reporting style.

- Learn to be aware of the provost's nonverbal clues. For instance, if the provost starts gathering papers and looking at his or her phone, a meeting might be coming to a close. If the provost always sits at the front of the room, don't take that chair. Learn what it means when the provost becomes silent in a meeting. This could mean the provost is pondering on something or is becoming upset with what's taking place in the meeting.
- If you are in a meeting with the provost and other academic leaders, watch who the provost talks to the most. Listen for the tone of the provost's voice. Be cognizant of the atmosphere in the room. If the discussion revolves around a budget concern, this is not a time to make a joke.

With all of these suggestions coming at you about what you should do and possible things to say, this might be the right time to add a few reminders about what not to do in certain situations. When meeting with the provost either in a one-on-one meeting or with other academics, avoid

- saying you don't remember being given a particular task,
- telling the provost you didn't understand what he or she wanted you to do,
- giving excuses for why something didn't get done (just regroup and complete the tasks), and
- pretending to be a psychic with the ability to read the provost's mind.

LET'S LOOK BACK

From setting up your personal space to learning how to read the provost's actions, your success as an associate provost is in your hands. On some days, your list of things to do will be overwhelming and possibly unachievable. There are many times when meetings and special requests from the provost will interfere with your ability to complete any and all items on your to-do list.

As you and the provost start working with one another and after a certain amount of time, you will be able to read the provost so well that your thoughts will be in sync and you will have created an easy working relationship.

Just as a map to the fairgrounds helps visitors plan what to see and where to go, learning the ropes and being aware of those who work in and with the academic community requires time, tenacity, and, most of all, courage.

Hopefully, the advice and suggestions in this chapter and others, will help you in building relationships and finding personal successes.

LET'S TALK REAL WORLD

There is no way to really tell you what your first few days and weeks will be like when you join the ranks of those who serve in higher education, especially in administrative positions. These stories and suggestions and this advice offer you possibilities for responses and actions to take as you move in and out of your new role. You will have your own experiences and learning moments.

Getting your feet wet as a new associate provost may take a little time. As you work closely with the provost and become acquainted with being a member of university administration, you will need to create systems for yourself that help you stay organized, on time to meetings, and cognizant of the staff and faculty that comprise the university community.

In the real world of university administration, time is your friend and your enemy. As you leave your office, you might notice that your car is the only one left in the parking lot. Because of the many tasks that lay before you in a single day, you might drive into that same parking lot before any other car appears.

Most workdays last for eight hours. Hopefully, you will get all you need to do completed or at least get a good start on what you need to do in those eight hours. Folks will walk right by your door on their way home, and you will still be trying to decipher a particular problem, one that the provost recently handed you.

Not all days will be quite as long, and not all of your time will be devoted to chores given by the provost. You will probably be responsible for other departments as well. The needs of those departments will also be time consuming. Remember, time can be your friend or your enemy. Set a schedule, work within time frames, and complete most (all) of your projects on time.

When you get into the office and begin your new day, the first thing you might do is open your emails. That's when your day changes, sometimes dramatically. There might be an email from the provost that redirects your entire day with an additional meeting or a new request. You may be directed to help in addressing a parent or student complaint, or a certain department under your purview might need your attention. There is really no way to prepare yourself for some of the changes that might take place.

So, what is the real world when you become an associate provost? You might be able to find a listing of the duties expected for an associate provost on any university web page. Most of these tasks describe the day-to-day activities associated with the role. Usually, there will be one major task that reads, "and all other duties as assigned." This catchall phrase encompasses many of your duties. Be prepared for any kind of change that might happen to the day you planned. Regroup, reorganize, and replan your day accordingly.

WHAT WOULD YOU DO?

Being in a leadership position at an institution of higher education requires your complete attention. If you have held previous leadership positions, you know that the best way to learn is by doing. For this reason and others, scenarios have been added throughout and at the end of each chapter for you to practice making decisions and choosing action steps that might help resolve the situation presented. Below is one such scenario.

At your first academic meeting with the provost, deans, and directors, you make a terrible mistake. You sit in the wrong place at the meeting table. What you didn't know is that seats at the table were unofficially assigned to specific deans and directors. When the would-be chair owner comes into the room, he announces that you are in the wrong seat and asks you to move. Being the new kid, you apologize for the mistake and move to the other side of the table without asking any questions.

In an effort to play nice with others at your first academic meeting, you moved. What you might not be aware of is that sitting near the provost allows you to share information when needed and answer any questions that the provost may have. What different actions do you think you might take to address this situation? The action steps are in no particular order.

- __ Ask the provost's administrative assistant if there are any other procedures or protocols that are in place for attending academic meetings.
- __ Ask for an agenda for the meeting as early as possible to familiarize yourself with the topics for that meeting.
- __ If you do make a protocol mistake early on, make an apology. You won't make the same mistake twice.
- __ When you are unfamiliar with a topic (such as a state or federal guideline) being discussed, make a note to yourself to explore that topic.
- __ Arrive at the meeting at least fifteen minutes early to secure your place at the table.

Chapter 2

Planning a Day at the Fair (Learn to Make Decisions)

The purpose of any map is to help someone get from a beginning point to a specific location. A map lists the specific roads and highways as well as the many cities and towns that are located along the way. When you choose a particular path, you don't know if you will encounter road construction, street closures, or detours. To get to the final destination, you will need to make some decisions. These decisions will make your drive easier, save you time, and help you reach your destination.

Receiving a map when you went through the gates at the State Fair of Texas was just the beginning of your day at the fair. The map detailed the location of the various exhibits, the food vendors, and the Midway, from which the laughter and screams of people playing games and riding rides can be heard throughout the park.

Using the map as a guide, you must make several decisions. What exhibit should you see first? Should you get something to eat before or after riding rides? Do you play games before or after visiting the petting zoo? There are so many places to see and so many things to do, and you have only one day.

As you view the map, you set a strategic plan in place. You consider when to visit the food vendors in order to avoid long lines at lunchtime. You take into consideration that the exhibit halls are always full when it is raining or too hot to be walking around the park. The decisions you make will help you see as much of the fair as possible. Your decisions also will help you be fed faster and to stand in lines less.

The map may serve as a guide for you, but you still are responsible for making certain decisions about the paths you want to take. For instance, if you have a craving for a corny dog and a large lemonade and you have only a short time before the next circus show starts, you might want to find a restroom. If you happen to be on one side of the fair, away from the closest restroom, a problem might ensue. With your handy-dandy map in hand, that possible problem may be avoided.

Before you buy that corny dog and large lemonade, you might choose to visit the Automobile Building. Is that the right decision? Should you see new cars before having something to eat or drink? Is the route you take to get to the Automobile Building a faster route to buying that corny dog? Before you take that next step, you have already mentally created a plan of action.

Having a map in hand is the perfect tool for getting around the fair. Unfortunately, there really is no map available for you when you become an associate provost and you are expected to have competent decision-making skills. Learning how to create an action plan and make "good" decisions are essential skills you will need as you create your own path as an associate provost.

DEFINING "GOOD" DECISIONS

All your life, you have been told by parents, grandparents, and teachers alike to think about what you were doing and to make good decisions. "You should be home before dark." "Be sure to take your vitamins every day." "For heaven's sake, don't walk under an open ladder." Even parts of a family or a school's discipline plan repeat the same dialogue over and over again, for example, Did you make a good decision?" Even when you were asked that question, there was still one more to answer. How did you learn to make what is considered a good decision?

When you are an associate provost, making good decisions is not an option; it is a must. Decisions at the level of the associate provost aren't always easy, and some have to be made at a moment's notice. Utpal Dholakia, in his article for *Psychology Today* (July 9, 2017 paragraph 17,), defines a good decision as one "that is made deliberately and thoughtfully, considers and includes all relevant factors, is consistent to the individual's philosophy and values, and can be explained clearly to significant others." In his definition of the factors that make up what a good decision should be, Dholakia details key points for you to remember as you begin making decisions, especially good ones, as an associate provost. Paraphrasing from the definition, Dholakia says good decisions are

- deliberate,
- thoughtful,
- encompass relevant factors,
- consistent, and
- clearly explainable.

While this list of attributes is not all-inclusive, you should consider these attributes when you are put in a position to make decisions. So, here's what you can do. Take these attributes, write them on an index card, and carry that index card with you at all times. When a decision has to be made, pull the card out of your pocket, read the list, and make your decision. Will this process work for you? The simple answer is no. The factors above must be ingrained in your thought processes and as natural to you as brushing your teeth.

As you begin learning what factors make up a good decision, you also must be on guard as to what factors might result in your making poor decisions. Poor decision-making at the university level can lead to situations that require legal involvement, that cause financial problems, or that create concerns between institutions. Not making poor decisions is as important as making good ones for your future as a successful associate provost. Utpal Dholakia provides several characteristics of what good decisions look like. Mike Erwin, in his 2019 article "6 Reasons We Make Bad Decisions and What To Do About Them," provides insight into what is taking place when leaders make bad decisions. Erwin states that leaders make bad decisions when

- they are tired,
- they become distracted,
- they lack pertinent and reliable data,
- they are multitasking, or
- they are emotionally tied to the decision.

Erwin's list also gives you some very valuable advice for making good decisions. Basically, he is saying don't make hasty decisions, use ample data to make the right decisions, and be sure to separate your emotions from the decision you have to make. Erwin's list describes the setting for poor decision-making. These identifiers will serve as possible guides for you when you start making decisions at your new level of responsibility. Remaining aware of these factors as you make decisions is nonnegotiable. You have to make good decisions.

In some instances, you may feel pressured to make a decision. Maybe a dean or a director wants you to make a decision "right here and right now." When this happens and you are the new guy in town, you need a few come-back statements that show you're sensitive to meeting the needs of an academic as well as to retaining your standing with the provost.

Your comments could and should include

- the fact that you are not going to make a decision without the provost's knowledge,
- your willingness to bring the request to the provost,

- the fact that any decision that is made will be made on the basis of research and the collection of relevant data,
- your willingness to move the issue forward to those who can be most helpful, and
- a request for understanding as the provost and his or her team works toward finding a solution.

However you choose to respond to those who ask you to make an immediate decision, be sincere and truthful about your ability to provide a solution.

PUTTING THIS INTO PRACTICE

Let's say the provost has given you the authority to make a decision about a particular curriculum issue. All the provost asks is that you keep him or her informed about the issue. If you use the factors of good decision-making previously mentioned, the scenario below might actually take place.

A dean wants to use a vacant faculty line to hire an assistant professor for a course. The course, at this time, has only thirty-six students enrolled in the two sections that are offered. The dean believes that enrollment for that course will increase and that a new section will be needed. The dean would like to offer another section and assign the newly hired assistant professor to the course.

Let's review a couple of very important decision-making tips.

- Don't make a decision under pressure.
- Gather as much data as possible.
- Make the decision that is in the best interests of the university.

Consider the above tips before you make one decision regarding the dean's request, and think about taking the following steps.

- After the dean makes the request to use the vacant faculty line to hire additional faculty, look not only at the current enrollment but also at what previous enrollment trends have been for this particular course to determine if, in fact, another faculty member is needed. You can request historical information about the course from the university department that is concerned with institutional research.
- From the same research department, ask for credentials of other faculty members in that particular college to determine if there is another faculty member who might be accredited to take on the extra course. This might

alleviate the need to hire additional personnel, thereby saving a dean's personnel line and an additional employment cost to the university.
* Determine if the course is connected to other degree plans.
* Determine if the course is a prerequisite for another program. Basically, determine if the requested course is important to other programs outside the college.

What do you really need to know about the steps mentioned above? In making a decision on this particular request from a dean, you should really know the following tidbits of information.

* Faculty lines are precious. Deans are usually very careful on how they use their open lines.
* A professor has to be credentialed to teach a class. If not, this could affect the accreditation of the entire program and, sometimes, of the university as a whole.
* The actual need for the course has to be determined. If enrollment for the course cannot be substantiated, the request should be denied.
* Degree plans for one program often call for courses in another program. When making curriculum or personnel changes, both programs have to be involved in the decision-making process.

Even though the provost gave you the authority to make some decisions, you should provide the provost with all the information you discover for his or her consideration. You can always provide the provost with some suggestions or recommendations on what you might do. But, as always, the final decision rests with the provost.

As a newly appointed associate provost, you may not be aware of the past history that exists between the dean and the provost. Just make sure the information and data you collect are clear and explainable to the dean if the request is denied. When any request, whether from a dean or any other academic, is denied, keep the collected data handy just in case you have to have a response. By doing your research, collecting valuable information, and presenting that information in a logical and well-thought-out plan, you will show the provost you have the ability to make good, solid decisions that benefit the university.

You should also be prepared to face faculty and staff members when a request they made has been denied, especially if you were the person they came to for assistance. Just as you would deliver any unpopular decision, be considerate, ask how else you might be able to help, and let them know you are willing to work with them to find another solution.

TIMING IS EVERYTHING

Decisions about where to park on the campus or what to wear to the board of regents' meeting are definitely decisions that require a thought process but are not decisions that will shake the halls of the university administration offices. Many decisions at the university level have a designated time limit and must be completed in a timely manner.

Decisions with a tight time frame usually revolve around the formation and closing out of budgets, the selection of curriculum for courses and programs in future semesters, the resolution of personnel issues, and the review of university policies. What you need to remember is that there are university, state, and federal timelines that have to be considered.

If you are not yet familiar with certain time limits that impact university operations, here are a few that are important for you to know and remember:

- At the end of an academic year, the university is responsible for providing a balanced budget to the state. This means that the various colleges and departments on the campus have to have a balanced budget to present to the provost for review. If a college is unable to balance its budget, the college may have to forfeit a faculty line or lose its travel monies to balance the budget. Regardless, the process at the end of the academic year must result in a balanced budget.
- At the same time of the year when the budget from the previous academic year has to be balanced, deans are required to submit their budgets for the next academic year. This is not a happy time for academic leaders. When deans and directors are given their possible budgets for the next academic year, they must decide how those funds are to be dispersed. This proposed budget also has to be approved by the provost.
  - **Point to Ponder**: Deans do not present their budgets to the president. The provost presents the deans' budgets to the president. This is why this process is so important to the provost. You might be asked to help with this issue. Be prepared for the gnashing of teeth and hair pulling that may take place in the closing out of one budget and the creation of a new one.
- Most universities have a policy regarding the process for and the time frame in which new academic programs can be added, modified, or deleted. Usually, there is a university committee that is in charge of the process. Once again, the provost has to review the recommendations before presenting them to the board of regents for final approval.
- The board of regents has to approve all curriculum decisions before they can be implemented through the modification of course and program

offerings. Because the board of regents has designated meeting times during the year, curriculum requests have to be presented and approved before the fall semester.

- **Point to Ponder:** In some cases, an associate provost is involved with curriculum issues. Even with university policies in place, some academic departments miss the deadlines and ask for special consideration. Do your homework. If the college or department has a habit of waiting to make its curriculum changes and of not following the due dates stated in the policy, the provost may send you to deliver the not-so-good news that its curriculum requests for that year will be denied since it did not meet policy deadlines.

- When a college or department decides to add a program (not necessarily a course), the university must approve the recommendation and then the newly designed program has to be approved at the state level (usually by a state board of higher education).

- Personnel issues usually are resolved at the university level. However, state accreditation guidelines require instructors and professors to be vetted properly. Basically, this means that a person who is assigned to teach a course at the higher education level must have the credentials to teach that course. The list of courses that are being offered at the university and the corresponding list of personnel who are assigned to teach those courses are submitted to the state for review on a continual basis. As mentioned before, failure to comply with this requirement could affect the university's accreditation.

- Textbook adoptions are definitely tied to a specific timeline. This particular deadline is due to the fact that a bookstore manager can purchase more used books when orders are placed early, which results in a reduced textbook cost to the students. If the deadline is not met, a bookstore manager may not have the opportunity to order more used books and may have to buy more new books, which affects the amount that students are charged for their books.

  - **Point to Ponder:** Your university may not have a specific policy regarding a deadline for ordering textbooks. If not, you might want to meet with the bookstore manager and learn about the textbook ordering process and how you can be of assistance.

- University policies are reviewed on a continual basis. As an associate provost who has to deal with a variety of issues, you will live and breathe in the land of policies. Policy revisions, deletions, or additions usually move through an approval process ending in the office of the provost. The final policy approval comes from the board of regents and only the board of regents.

- **Point to Ponder**: After every board of regents' meeting, a listing of policies under review should be included in the meeting minutes. Because policies often affect the academic side of the house, you may want to pay close attention to policy changes that take place.

Decisions in the area of higher education move slowly through several processes. Then, when deadlines are approaching, people from all parts of the university start to scramble to make sure certain deadlines are met. Decisions to accept late requests usually fall to the provost who, in turn, may turn that decision over to you. Again, be prepared to be the deliverer of some not-so-good news.

Here is just a word of advice: If, in your role as associate provost, you are handed a project of any kind, always ask about the deadline and due dates. If possible, when you find out when something is due, backtrack at least five days and make that your personal due date. Please reread the first few words in that last sentence, and let "if possible" become your new mantra. You must become a master scheduler and planner of your time or due dates will get away from you before you know it.

Piyush Goyal, the Indian Minister of Commerce and Industry, said, "The speed of decision making is the essence of good governance" (http://brainyquotes.com/quotes/piyush_goyal_846703). This quote reminds you that making good decisions in a timely manner helps to protect the academic community and to establish governance practices. Making good decisions in a timely manner also helps to establish your currency as a credible associate provost.

CREATING A PERSONAL DECISION-MAKING STYLE

If there was a magical looking glass and you could see into the future, hopefully you would see yourself as a successful associate provost, surrounded by administrators, academics, faculty members, and staff members that make effective decisions. If you are surrounded by colleagues who make effective decisions, borrow a few of their skills and begin the process of developing your own personal decision-making style.

Tony Robbins, known for his personal empowerment coaching skills, says, "It is in your moment of decision making that your destiny is shaped" (brainyquotes.com/topics/decision-quotes). Robbins is correct in his prediction that, when you make decisions, you actually forecast your future in your role as an associate provost.

Will you make good and great decisions every time? Hopefully. Will all of your decisions be based on policies and in the best interests of the university?

Always. Is making good and valued decisions a learned skill? Yes. Does the provost expect this to be one of your best skills? Most definitely.

Some of your colleagues may use the old "go with the gut" style of decision-making. They let their feelings guide their decisions. Think back to the Erwin article that mentions what happens when you let emotions guide your decisions. Not all of those decisions will be good ones. Since you might be fairly new to the workings of higher education and you might be brand new to the institution, your "gut" may be doing somersaults—take an antacid. However, for heaven's sake, don't make decisions using your gut.

Avoid making decisions when you are upset or in a bad mood. Most of these decisions will come back to haunt you. You never want the provost to lose faith in your decision-making skills. Having conversations with the provost after you have made a poor decision could be difficult for you. Avoid making poor decisions at all costs.

If you find yourself in a bad mood or you become upset with a situation that has taken place, take a walk around the campus. Leave your office. Grab a hamburger. Take yourself away from the situation for a few minutes. And, most importantly, avoid making important decisions when you are in this frame of thought.

Developing a personal decision-making style oftentimes means that you find a person whose decision-making style you would like to emulate. This might mean you watch the provost or another administrator make decisions. Listen to the way others respond when presented with decision-making responsibilities. Look for a person who remains calm in the face of dilemmas. Such people usually make good decisions. They wait until they have viable and reliable data to respond to certain questions. Learn from them. Quiet, calm decision-making may serve you well.

Whatever decision-making style you create, be sure it is a lasting one. Quite simply, your decision-making style needs to be consistent and known to all, especially the provost. Creating your particular style of decision-making will take some time. Making your style known to the academic community will take more time, because not all of your decisions will be seen by the academic community as a whole. You want those you work with to be as familiar with how you approach a situation as you are.

As you begin to form your own decision-making style, remember these points:

- Keep the system simple. What's the problem? Who needs to be talked to? When is a decision needed? Simple.
- Collect as much data as possible. Most of your decisions should be data driven.

- Create a template, either on paper or using technology, that helps you keep track of the information you have gathered. Avoid using yellow sticky notes, especially when reporting back to the provost about a decision you made.
- Don't be afraid or worried about asking for help when making decisions. If others help or provide assistance in this learning process, be sure to thank them.
- Find people who are in key positions around the campus and whom you trust to be truthful when you ask for information.
- After a decision has been made, be sure to check back with those who made the request to ask if they need anything else.
- Always, always, keep the provost informed about the decisions that you made.

The most common reminder you have noticed in these first two chapters centers on your keeping the provost notified and aware of many aspects of your job as the associate provost. This doesn't mean that you send him a diary log of everything you have done. The provost has given you a job and expects you to do it and do it well. Don't forget: If you think you are busy, the provost is even busier. You can simply ask the provost how he or she would like to be informed about any situation. All that is needed might be a short email.

Developing a decision-making style of your own may seem like a simple task. Many decisions at your level of administration require immediate responses. Deans, directors, and faculty wait anxiously for personnel and budgetary decisions. Students who have asked you for decisions regarding their grades or discipline situation tend to become very anxious in their wait. Your style should mirror efficiency and appropriateness, and your process should be easily communicated and follow university policies.

YOUR DECISIONS AND THE IMPACT THEY HAVE

Imagine for one moment that you are standing near a beautiful forest and at the edge of the forest is a calm, serene lake. You pick up a rock and throw it into the lake. As soon as you do that, the ripples in the water begin. You stand at the edge of the lake until you can't see even the smallest ripple take place.

Not being able to see the last ripple in the lake is exactly what it is like not knowing how your decisions impact others and the entire academic community. Developing a personal decision-making style is not the only thing you must keep in mind. You must also be aware of the impact of your decisions.

- The decisions you make for students have to be carefully considered because the academic future of the student is at stake. A student may have to sit out a semester, take courses over again, or delay his or her graduation. The decisions you make for a student could impact university enrollment and program offerings.
- The decisions you make for staff and faculty, whether concerning personnel or curriculum, could impact every department and college at the university. Program and course approvals might be delayed. Personnel might not be hired on time.
- The decisions you make for the academic community could affect the culture and climate of the university. Policies might not be followed, which could potentially lead to legal issues. Decisions you make could impact the relationships you are trying to build within the institution.
- The decisions you make for the provost could affect your relationship with the provost. So, make good and deliberate decisions.

Keeping in mind the above suggestions about creating a personal decision-making style and the impact your decisions could make, consider using some of the following resources

- University policies
- Institutional research
- Historical data, verbal and written
- Department practices
- Faculty syllabi
- Student records
- University reporting schedules

As the associate provost, you will have access to all of the above resources. Use them, and ask for information from these areas to assist you in making good decisions.

SUGGESTIONS FOR BUILDING YOUR SKILLS IN DECISION-MAKING

This chapter focuses on the importance of making good decisions and suggests how you can strengthen your skills in decision-making. These skills will be essential to your success as an associate provost, and you will use these skills on a daily basis. Here are a few more important points to improve your decision-making skills:

- When you are faced with making a decision, first make sure you have the authority to make that decision and it falls under the purview of your position as associate provost. If you need to, have a conversation with the provost early in the decision-making process to clearly understand what authority you do have.
- When you are faced with an academic decision, be sure to check with the department and college to determine if any of the procedures they have in place might impact your decision.
- If an academic associate or friend contacts you for a "favor" that involves making a decision in that person's favor, telling that person no or that you can't help them at this particular time is better than explaining a poor decision you made to the provost.
- If you have collected all the data you need and are ready to make a good decision, make it and stand by it. You've done your homework. One of the worst mistakes you can make is to be seen as a wishy-washy decision maker.
- When you make a decision and you are presenting that decision to the provost, avoid telling the provost what to do. Instead, just present the provost with some suggestions and recommendations and let the provost know you will follow his or her lead.
- When making decisions, consider listening to an array of voices, possibly through some committees or a small group. The stakeholders involved in the decision should have a chance to be heard since the decision will most likely impact their areas and practices.
- If an emergency arises and you must make an immediate decision, make the best possible decision you can to address the cares and concerns of others and the community as a whole. Because your role is an administrative role, you should considerfor the needs of the entire university.

Most of the decisions you make at your level will revolve around curriculum planning, student issues, and personnel concerns. When you create your personal decision-making style that works for you, you will become an asset to the organization and especially the provost. The provost needs to know you can be trusted to do the right thing for the right reasons.

LET'S LOOK BACK

Did you have a good day at the fair? Were you able to make a decision about where to go and what to do? Was the map helpful to you when making those decisions? Of course, it was. The map provided you with direct and indirect paths to get you where you needed to be.

Making decisions will come more easily to you once you face the many decisions that will fall into the area of an associate provost. With the information, examples, and suggestions provided in this chapter, hopefully the decisions you make for others will support the mission of your institution and the needs of the academic community.

LET'S TALK ABOUT THE REAL WORLD

You may already be quite adept at making decisions. Some of the situations you face will require a simple yes or no as a response. On the other hand, some that you face will be extremely difficult. Telling a student that he or she cannot return to the campus because of grades or behaviors is not easy. Informing parents that their son or daughter will not be graduating is difficult. Informing a dean or director that a request for another position cannot be approved at this time is challenging. These are only a few of many difficult decisions that might come your way.

The suggestions and recommendations in this chapter have several common themes. Those themes include consistency, policy awareness, and communication. You might think you are only building a decision-making style, but you also are really establishing your ability to make good decisions.

WHAT WOULD YOU DO?

The scenario below could actually be a situation you encounter during the first few years of service to the university. After reading the scenario, you will see some possible steps you could take to render a workable solution. Read through the steps and determine what process would work for you. The listing of action steps is not in any particular order.

You and the provost are in discussions about the budget for a department assigned to you. It appears that the department has more staff members than is necessary. The provost has charged you with reducing the number of personnel in that department as a savings measure. You already know this department has a few difficult staff members and this decision must be carefully planned out. The provost needs your decision in one week.

Possible Actions
- __ Decide which the positions to eliminate.
- __ Review existing personnel positions.
- __ Review the departmental budget.
- __ Review the existing duties of personnel.

- __ Arrange a meeting with the department director to address the situation.
- __ Ask the provost how much money needs to be saved to balance the budget.
- __ Meet with the personnel in the department to inform them of the budget reductions.
- __ Meet with the personnel in the department to inform them of the final decision.
- __ Meet with the provost when the decision to reduce the number of personnel is made.

The exercise above shows a few options for you to consider taking when making decisions that involve a directive from the provost, a budget reduction, and personnel issues. While the listing above is of actual steps to take and the steps are listed in no particular order, you will be the one responsible for making the best decision possible. You know what to do.

Chapter 3

You've Been to the Fair Before (Reviewing What You Should Already Know)

The State Fair of Texas, located in Dallas, Texas, is one of the biggest events that hits the city. In addition to the many events that occur and the many exhibits that are open during the fair, the traditional football game between Oklahoma University and the University of Texas takes place. The Cotton Bowl is filled with thousands of fans from both sides.

If Oklahoma wins the game, the fans from Texas tend to go home. If Texas wins, those fans tend to stay at the fair and mobs of winning fans flood the fair. Because this game has been played between Oklahoma University and the University of Texas since 1929, you can imagine the numbers of fans that come to the game every year. A sea of orange and maroon fills every lane, street, and path of the fairgrounds. While this game is playing, the fairgrounds are basically empty—until the game is over. Then, the population of people at the fair changes dramatically.

As mentioned, if Texas wins the game, the fans stay around, buy a lot of adult beverages, and crowd every area of the fair. If Oklahoma wins, many of the Texas fans leave the fair and the fair fills up with Oklahoma fans who then crowd the fair's pathways and buy more adult beverages.

If you plan on visiting the fair during the Cotton Bowl weekend, you really need to know what is going to happen before, during, and after the game. You already have mastered the use of the fair's map, and you know how to navigate through the Midway and where the corny dogs are sold. So, with the knowledge you have, you set a plan in place. The game will last at least three hours, so you can see all of the exhibits, grab a bite to eat, and even take a break at the reflection pond.

The Cotton Bowl weekend is the one weekend during the fair season when you should know what is going on and use that knowledge to plan accordingly. Just as you have prior knowledge of what is going to happen at the State Fair of Texas during Cotton Bowl weekend, you already possess some prior knowledge of the many issues that will arise in the administration of an institution of higher education, especially issues that relate to your role as an associate provost.

For instance, you already know that you will be in a position of leadership, that you will have a long list of duties and responsibilities, that the provost is expecting you to handle any situation that comes your way, and that everyday your position will take you someplace new.

YOUR STRENGTHS

Among the candidates that applied for the position of associate provost, you were the one chosen to hold the position. Through meetings and the interview process, you exhibited traits or characteristics that demonstrated you had the skills to be a valued member of the administration of a university, you possessed the ability to build lasting relationships with members of the academic community and external constituents, and you can express your thoughts in a deliberate and concise manner. These are skills that you already have. So, you will already have some abilities to face the responsibilities of the associate provost. In John C. Maxwell's book, *The 21 Indispensable Qualities of Becoming a Leader: Becoming the Person Others Will Want to Follow* (1991), he lists twenty-one traits that leaders should possess.

Character	Listening
Charisma	Passion
Commitment	Positive Attitude
Communication	Problem Solving
Competence	Relationships
Courage	Responsibility
Discernment	Security
Focus	Self-Discipline
Generosity	Servanthood
Initiative	Teachability

VISION

Looking at this list of qualities, you might be wondering how some of these help to define successful leadership. What does security mean? Does generosity mean you give to the United Way Fund every year? While Maxwell does give a summary for each of these traits, you can also define each one of these for your role as an associate provost.

You probably have already noticed some of the traits are second nature to you. From your previous occupations or positions, you know you have courage to face difficult situations. Regardless of what happens in your day, you keep a positive attitude. The passion you have for your job reflects in everything you do, and your communication skills are stellar.

As you recognize the traits you already possess, you also have to reflect on some of the traits that you need to strengthen as you begin your role. Maybe you need to learn to be more focused when preparing a report or before speaking in a meeting? Should you be more charismatic when addressing deans and other faculty members? Do you possess a unique listening skill that enables you to act appropriately when given a new task?

While the list Maxwell provides is not an all-encompassing list of the qualities that you will need as you begin your tenure as a newly appointed associate provost, the qualities listed are a good place to start to identify the strengths you already possess. How does knowing strengths you already have as well as those you need to work on assist you in your role? The strengths you already have allow you to take on difficult situations that may come your way.

As you review the list of leadership qualities from your perspective, look at the list again from the viewpoint of the provost and his or her expectations of you and your ability to successfully complete each responsibility given to you.

When the provost looks at the trait of courage and thinks of you, the provost may not think you have the ability to run into a burning building to save a cat. The provost needs to see how you face difficult situations that arise between faculty members or the way you deliver not-so-good news to those in the academic community. The provost needs to know he or she can assign to you any particular task and you will not shirk any responsibility.

As the newly appointed associate provost, you have a lot to learn. You already know this. Leadership looks different at this administrative level. The actions you take in this role impact more than just those in your office. They could impact the entire academic community. Teachability refers to your willingness to adapt, learn new procedures and protocols, and take directions, when given, from the provost or other administrators.

Competence is THE trait the provost has to see in you through every accomplished task, every conversation you have, and every problem you solve. The provost has to know, when he or she gives you a job, that the job will be completed in the best way possible. You already possess skills and abilities that are beneficial to the provost or you wouldn't be in the position. In this new role, having competence is essential to keeping your position.

THE MEANING OF RESPONSIBILITY

If you are in the position of the associate provost, one of the first of many attributes you need to convey to the provost and other administrators is your ability to be responsible. Does this kind of responsibility translate into your ability to return library books on time? Does it mean that you adhere to the speed limit? No, this type of responsibility, at the level of the associate provost, means that you take care of the departments given to you and the personnel needs associated with each department, you won't overspend budget monies in your departments, and, when students reach out to you with academic needs, you do everything you can to help them.

The level of responsibility you will face on a daily basis is definitely not for the faint of heart and is sometimes daunting. However, you have the job, you came with ingrained skills, and tenure in your position will be long lasting as you face each situation that comes your way.

Responsibility is already one of your traits or you wouldn't be serving in a position of leadership at an institution of higher education. With this in mind, what other actions can you take that exemplify your ability to be responsible?

- Volunteer to attend a meeting for the provost if the provost is unable to attend and provide the provost with a summary of the meeting.
- Volunteer to mentor newly appointed administrators and to keep the provost informed about the progress they are making.
- Offer to assist other administrators if a situation arises in which you can be helpful and then follow through by providing the provost with a summary.
- When students need help with academic issues, serve as a conduit for them to the provost's office and other university offices.

You might be asking yourself why should you take on more responsibilities when your plate is already full? Is it really important to volunteer for extra duties when you can barely get through your own to-do list? The answer is most definitely. Every day you are working to build your credibility. Every day you are working to prove that you are the right person for the job and that the provost did not make a mistake in hiring you. Accepting other responsibilities is one way to do that.

Here is another reality point for you to remember. There is absolutely no benefit to you or your reputation to become a complainer about your workload or any new tasks that have been added to your list of things to do. Everyone that works at the university has a to-do list. Your colleagues' lists may not be as long as yours, but, nonetheless, your colleagues have tasks to accomplish. You have been entrusted with responsibilities, and the provost is counting on you to fulfill any assignment given to you.

Would it be wise to have a conversation with the provost when your plate is too full despite putting in ten-hour days, letting the provost know that you are overwhelmed and having a little trouble meeting all the demands of your position? How do you think that conversation is really going to go? Do you think the provost will tell you to take a couple of days off and rest up? Maybe the provost will say that he or she will take care of all of your responsibilities? That's probably not going to happen.

No matter how stressful things get, no matter how many tasks you are assigned, no matter the tasks on your own to-do list, accept the tasks that are handed to you and get the jobs done. Avoid complaining. It never looks pretty on anyone, especially someone with all the responsibilities you have.

Only you can define your growth and maturity in the area of responsibility. Your growth may be defined by the way you take care of your departments and their people. Your maturity level may be defined by the way you complete projects or tasks. Here are a few other ways your level of responsibility will be recognized by others and as well as yourself:

- Whatever you are responsible for, own it. Whether your responsibility is for a department, staff members, or decisions made by others, the "buck stops with you," so to speak.
- Try not to put too many tasks on your to-do list, especially on days when you have meetings. You may walk away from a meeting with more things to do.
- Schedule meetings with the departments under your purview every other week. You need to touch base with the faculty and staff in these areas as often as possible. Maintaining communication with these departments prevents unwanted surprises.
- What the provost asks you to take care of should be your priority.
- When asked to lead or serve in a position to represent the university, accept. Networking with other administrators in higher education is essential.
- Choose a day for yourself, block it out on your calendar, and stand by it. Everyone needs time to refresh and reload.
- Find a person, usually your highly efficient administrative assistant, to whom you feel comfortable delegating tasks. Regardless of what you feel you can give that person, you will still be responsible for the outcome.

From what you have read so far about taking care of responsibilities given to you as an associate provost, you may envision an associate provost as someone who wears a red cape and can stop a runaway train. Taking on extra responsibilities and completing those tasks also provides you with opportunities to develop your sense of responsibility to the fullest.

LEVELS OF CONFIDENCE

Being an associate provost requires—almost mandates—you to possess a level of confidence to do your job. Don't confuse being confident with being cocky; these are two different things entirely. Every time you accomplish a task in the manner and according to the timeline given to you by the provost, your level of confidence increases. Every time you help a student with an academic need and it helps the student stay in school, you should pat yourself on the back and tell yourself, "Job well done." These situations are confidence builders.

So, how does having confidence differ from being cocky? When faced with an academic problem or situation, a confident person can provide a viable solution, problem solved—that's confidence. Walking around the campus crowing about your accomplishments is being cocky. Being cocky doesn't look good on anyone, especially anyone who serves in administration.

The Maxwell list of characteristics and traits all leaders should have does not but should include confidence. Confidence happens when you accept the fact that you can do your job and do it well. What actions can you take to help build the trait of confidence?

- Every time you meet with a disgruntled faculty member and you help solve a situation, recognize your ability to problem solve.
- Every time you meet a deadline, especially with time to spare, take yourself out to lunch.
- Every time you are able to help a student, especially a junior or senior, stay in school, celebrate. It doesn't matter how.
- Every time you find an open parking space on campus, yell, "woo hoo!" as loudly as you can and pull into the empty space as quickly as you can.

Remember, it's the little celebrations that mean the most and help build your confidence level and keep you on this side of cockiness. Additionally, the provost will be watching as your confidence level grows. Have faith that, regardless of what the provost gives you to do, you will come out ahead.

Being new to the realm of leadership at the associate provost's level doesn't mean you have a low level of confidence. It simply means that you have new responsibilities and answer to university administrators. These old sayings might actually serve as starting points for growth in confidence:

- If it ain't broke, don't fix it. When you develop a system to address problem situations and that system works, keep it.
- Developing a successful system to address any situation is a confidence builder.
- Speak softly and carry a big stick. Whenever you can resolve a situation in a quick and quiet manner, you will not have to pull the "I am an associate provost and you're not" card. You won't need that particular big stick. This is definitely a confidence builder.
- Let sleeping dogs lie. If there is a particularly difficult situation and others want to include you (as well as your position) in that situation, let sleeping dogs lie. Where appropriate, be strong enough to walk away and let others solve the problems for themselves. In this way, you are allowing others to grow in their confidence.
- How do you eat an elephant? One bite at a time. When you are faced with larger-than-life projects, problems, or situations, it might seem like they all have to be solved immediately. You might start thinking you don't have what it takes, you can't possibly get all the answers you need, or it's just too much. That's because you are looking at the elephant. Break down the situations into parts or tasks and, after each is solved, pat yourself on the back, and take another bite. You will get more confident with each bite.
- Some days you're the bug, some days you're the windshield. According to conventional wisdom, this lyric written by Dire Straits means that sometimes you find yourself powerless (i.e., the bug) and in the hands of more powerful forces (i.e., the windshield).
- Sometimes the reverse is true. However, another way you may interpret this saying is to empower the bug and view the bug as having agency and the ability to plan and to choose a safe path. Similarly, you may disempower the windshield and view it as lacking agency and as being passive, simply encountering situations as they occur, without preparation.
- Consider looking at this saying in that way and choosing to be the bug that plans and prepares rather than being the passive windshield. For every victory, no matter how small, celebrate a little, walk a little taller, and fill up your confidence reservoir. You should set a goal of having more bug days than windshield days.

THE SOFT SKILLS

In an article by Alison Doyle, *What are the Soft Skills* (July, 2022), she stated the following:

Soft skills relate to how you work/Soft skills include interpersonal skills, people skills, communication skills, listening skills, time management, and empathy for others. They are among the top skills employers seek in the candidates they hire, because soft skills are important for just about every job.

The soft skills mentioned above are some of the skills that you brought to the table when you accepted the position of associate provost. Surely your communication skills were evident during the interview process. Your responses must have expressed how you would care for the university and its people. So, how will you show the provost and other administrators that you have the listening and time-management skills needed for your position?

You will not believe how important the skill of listening will be in your role. There are a few ways that you can use the skill of listening in your position. There is the act of nodding your head in agreement and all the while thinking of what you need from Walmart. Then, there is attending. This is the kind of listening where you put down what you are working on, turn around from your computer, and give your full attention to the speaker.

Another, sometimes-forgotten form of listening is to stop talking and watch what is happening around you. Listening, in this form, is oftentimes the most difficult because it means you have to give your full attention to what is happening around you. This skill is especially important during meetings. What are some ways you can develop these types of listening?

- You may not believe this, but your ability to listen to someone is associated with your energy level. For instance, if you are a morning person, consider scheduling as many meetings as you can in the morning. The same thing applies if your energy level is highest in the afternoon. Avoid scheduling meetings after lunch, if possible. You already know you might be nodding off during such a meeting.
- When someone visits your office and you know they really need you to listen to a need or concern they have, drop everything you are working on, grab a pen and paper, and focus on the visitor. If that person has taken the time to visit your office and has a concern, especially one you can help with, it's time for that person to have your complete attention.
- When the provost talks, you always listen. If the provost conducts a meeting and you are unable to attend (you might be at a conference), see if the meeting is going to be taped and ask if the link can be sent to you. The same procedures should apply if a meeting takes place with other administrators. Try your best to stay as knowledgeable as you can regarding university happenings.

- When having conversations, especially with the provost, feel free to interrupt the conversation to clarify what is being asked of you. This will save you a great deal of time and bring needed clarity to your next assignment. As your listening skills improve, you won't have to interrupt too often.
- If you are new to the campus and you start the process of meeting as many staff members as possible, be attentive to the information they share. Consider, after you meet this staff member and have a conversation about his or her family, responsibilities at the university, or favorite place to eat, taking notes. Save the information on your phone or create a file on your computer. By listening to the folks and then remembering what they shared with you for your next conversation, you will go a long way in developing positive relationships with those on the campus.
- If you are in a meeting and the conversation turns serious, stop what you're doing and start listening to what is taking place. Listen to the conversations taking place in the room. Watch the interaction taking place. Take notes if you have to, but stay attentive.

If you currently consider yourself a good listener, keep up the good work. This is one skill that is essential to your work with the provost and to the completion of your duties and responsibilities.

The art of time management, and it will become an art, has and will continue to be discussed throughout the chapters. Think about time management as one of the soft skills that you need in your position. Having time-management skills will help you to recognize how much time you have at your disposal to address concerns, solve problems as they come to you, and take care of the departments and people under your purview.

Does being a good time manager mean you won't have time for lunch unless you schedule it? No, that's not it.

Does being a good time manager mean you could forget to attend a meeting if it's not scheduled? Possibly.

Will some days provide you with more time than you thought you would have? Sure. Meetings can be canceled, visitors who want to see you will change their minds, and you may finish a project early. With your skills of time management, you might want to use this newly found free time to move to the next project that the provost has given you. You might want to take an opportunity to visit faculty and staff across the university. Having time-management skills means that you know how to use your time wisely and to help you complete your many assigned tasks.

In her 2022 article, Doyle mentions the skill of empathy. The term "empathy" means the action of or capacity to feel for others, to put yourself in their shoes, to feel what they are experiencing. As an administrator for the university and as a decision maker on the campus, what does empathy mean in your service to the institution?

- When working with students who have serious academic concerns, lose the phrase, "I understand what you are going through." No, you don't. It may have been a while since you were in college and failing a class. It may have been a while since you didn't have any money to stay in school. It may have been a while since you couldn't get a class you needed to graduate. Instead, try the phrase, "Let me see what I can do to help."
- When working with deans and faculty members and they bring a problem to your attention, don't hand it off to someone else. Basically, you are the someone else. Use every resource you have, make the connections that are needed, and resolve as much of the problem you can. When you have this kind of situation, don't make any promises. You will be concerned for the academic community, but don't assume the problem is all yours.
- When parents call and want a helping hand, you can listen to their needs, you can gather some information, but remember not to say you understand what they are going through. You don't. They might not be able to get to their child to help them. You might be their only connection to the academic side of the house. As with other situations, tell the parents you do care what happens to their child and you are going to help as much as possible.

These are only a few of the many times you will be called on to have a sense of empathy for those in the university community. Of course, you want to be helpful. Of course, you want to be considerate of others' feelings and needs. That's empathy, and this soft skill is always needed.

LET'S LOOK BACK

By using Maxwell's list of characteristics as a gauge for your leadership development and to maintain your leadership abilities, you may have found some hidden talents.

You might have taken a moment to look inward at your own strengths and limitations. Hopefully, you will also come to realize how the role of the associate provost requires some kind of action from you every day.

So here you are, a newly hired associate provost. You've gained many strengths and abilities as you moved in and out of your academic assignments.

Here are a few suggestions to make both your strengths and limitations work for you as you serve the academic community:

- When you recognize a strength, use that strength all the time. For instance, if your strength is problem-solving, be prepared to be called upon to use that skill either by the provost or another university administrator.
- If you find yourself limited in the area of servanthood, for instance, seek others who will serve as examples for you and help you grow in this skill.

Basically, let the identified skills that you are good at work for you and work on the ones that need to be developed.

Whether you are visiting the State Fair of Texas on Cotton Bowl weekend or beginning your journey as a new associate provost, the skills and abilities you already possess will see you through. Whether you are maneuvering through a sea of orange and white shirts at the fair or are getting through your first academic meeting as an associate provost, the ability to use your skills wisely will serve you well.

Regardless of the number of times you have been to the State Fair of Texas, you have a basic understanding of what takes place. You know there will be new and good foods to try, there will be rides and games on the Midway, and there will be plenty of exhibits to see. Just as you know your way around the fairgrounds, in the university setting, you have some basic leadership skills and abilities that will help you do your job well and will assist you in building positive relationships with the provost and others in the academic community.

LET'S TALK ABOUT THE REAL WORLD

Having and showing your abilities and strengths will certainly help you in your new role. In the real world, this could also be a liability. When you are good at something, as mentioned previously, you will be called on constantly to solve the type of problem that you are skilled at solving. Here's the quandary: Being good at something sometimes means you are often—all the time—called upon to use that specific skill to benefit others.

So, where do you draw the line? Do you tell the provost or the president, "No," or "Wish I could help, but I'm just too busy right now," when they ask you to do something? Did you forget you are trying to build up your credibility with the academics across the campus? Did you forget you just got the position and telling the provost or any other administrator that you were too busy to help might lead to a short-term position?

When you are asked to help, when others come to you because of your super powers, something on your list of things to do gets pushed aside or meetings get rescheduled. Your to-do list starts looking a little impossible to complete. Continue to focus on building your credibility and finding a little balance in your work world.

WHAT WOULD YOU DO?

As an academic in an administrative position for an institution of higher education, you will have many opportunities to use the skills you already developed as an academic. The scenario provided below sets in place a situation you may encounter, a situation in which your skills will come into play. Several steps are added for your consideration. Read through the steps and determine which ones would work for you.

The steps are listed in no particular order.

After being named to the position of associate provost, the president informs you that one of the departments assigned to you is having a few problems with the administrative staff as well as with staff morale. The president asks you to address the situation because he or she has heard you are an effective communicator. To improve the current situation in this department, what would you do?

- __ Gather staff members together and ask them what is taking place in the department.
- __ Ask the administrative staff to provide you with a list of procedures and processes for each area of the department.
- __ Make an appointment with the administrative staff to ask what concerns they might have at this time.
- __ Schedule appointments with each staff member to discuss the morale situation in the department.
- __ Ask the staff member for suggestions on steps that could be taken to improve the morale of the department.
- __ Conduct before and after surveys to determine the morale status of the department.
- __ With the help of the administrative staff, establish some achievable and measurable goals to improve the relationships in the department.
- __ Set in place a few actions that were suggested by the staff members.

The above actions, although certainly not the only steps you could take to address the charge given to you by the president, will hopefully provide you with a few starting points. The president did not ask if you were inclined to solve the problem. The president did not tell you to call on him or her if you needed any assistance. Because the president had heard about or seen your ability to communicate with others and the department was assigned to you, you were put in charge. Your skill in communicating with others will have served you well, and, when the problem has been solved, you will have gained credibility with the president.

Chapter 4

Riding the Roller Coaster (Dealing with Politics in Higher Education)

Whether it is the Texas Tornado, the Giant Dipper, or the Boulder Dash, all roller coasters have the same things in common (kidadl.com/articles/roller-coaster-names-from-around-the world, n.d.). They all go fast, they all have twists and turns, and they all leave your stomach a bit queasy.

Here you are at the entrance to the roller coaster ride at the State Fair of Texas, deciding if you really want to take a chance on the ride. Fast rides have never been fun or exciting for you, and all of the screaming from the frantic riders is definitely not your thing. Are you ready to be thrown about, turned upside down, and possibly lose that corny dog you had for lunch? In the back of your mind, you know that a day at the fair is really not complete without riding rides, especially the scary roller coaster.

From across the fairgrounds, you have been able to hear the screams and yells of the riders. Even though you can see the twists and turns and you know the ride will go very fast, you have no idea about the intensity of the ride until you actually get on. Yet, there you stand in the line ready to hand over your tickets. The outcome is definitely unknown, but you are willing to take a chance on the ride. It really could be a lot of fun.

So it goes when you start working with university policies and the politics involved with institutions of higher education. You may have limited knowledge of what to expect when dealing with these aspects of higher education. The faster you learn about the politics and policies that guide the workings of a university the better.

LET'S TALK POLITICS

To understand the politics that takes place at an institution of higher education, you must first clear your mind of what you already know about politics or how you think politics works. The type of politics you will find at an institution of higher education is not associated with any particular party or specific political affiliations. This type of politics revolves around academic positions, existing university policies, and the workings of a board of regents.

Breaking this kind of politics down to a level that is relevant to you in your role as an associate provost, your political focus will address

- those who are in positions of authority and power,
- your place in the political arena,
- those who hold the **real** authority and power, and
- the importance of the chain of command.

Regardless of the positions you have held in the past and the political systems in those places, every workplace has its own political system and the university is no different. When dealing with employees, there are always mounds of paperwork that have to be completed even when hiring someone. There are always supervisors who hold positions of authority over workers. There are always queens and worker bees.

For example, at McDonald's, a new employee starts at the French fry station and is there until he can move up to building hamburgers. Employees at McDonald's must follow certain rules and procedures. Even when making hamburgers, there is a pattern to follow: "two all-beef patties, special sauce, lettuce, cheese, pickles, onions, on a sesame-seed bun" (https://www.nytimes .com). This particular system of making a hamburger has made the company millions of dollars.

Similarly, in a university, paperwork and positions make up only a couple of the aspects of what is involved in the workings of a political system. In a university's political system, and especially in the provost's office, known authoritative positions, departmental procedures, and state and federal guidelines must be followed.

You may not be making hamburgers and may not be in line to make millions of dollars, but you do stand in a political position. In your role, you may be responsible for several university programs or departments. The provost may ask you to assist with legal situations that take place. Be mindful of the fact that you will probably serve as a conduit between the academics of the campus and university administrators. Therefore, it is imperative you learn about the political system of academics and the political system of administrators.

THE POLITICAL SYSTEM OF A SPECIFIC
COLLEGE OR DEPARTMENT

If you have achieved the position of associate provost, you are probably already familiar with the fact that a dean leads each college. The dean, much like the principal of a school or the manager of a department store, is responsible for absolutely everything that happens in his or her college. The dean approves budgets, personnel choices, teaching assignments, course scheduling, and curriculum additions and deletions in the college and also handles any other concerns or problems that arise in the college.

The organizational chart that Chapter 1 suggested you use to start meeting staff and faculty members in the academic community makes clear that the provost is directly responsible for every dean in every college. In essence, this also means that the provost might call upon you to address a situation that arises with a dean or something that happens in a dean's college.

If you were a member of the faculty at the institution before accepting the position of associate provost, you have an advantage because you will be familiar with the deans, their departments, and, possibly, their faculty members. You might have worked with the deans and their faculty members previously on a project or might have seen their behaviors in meetings. This prior knowledge will be helpful for you in your new role.

However, if you are new to the university and have limited knowledge about a dean or his or her college, you might need another kind of map to be your guide. Think about the following as you learn how to work in a positive political atmosphere with the deans.

- During academic meetings with the provost and the deans, pay close attention to the conversations that take place between the provost and the deans. You will learn a great deal about the relationships that exists among them.
- If a dean asks you to intervene for him or her with the provost about any situation, make no promises. You may or may not know the type of relationship that exists between the two or how many times the dean and the provost had a conversation about the same issue. For instance, if the dean has asked the provost for additional personnel and the provost has denied the request, you do not want to be in the middle of that situation.
- If a faculty member asks you to intervene to his or her dean about a specific situation, see the above: same situation, same outcome.
- If a dean asks for a favor that is in your purview to make happen and you are able to fulfill the request, you will be in the dean's good graces.

The dean will remember your helpfulness, and your credibility with this dean and other deans will continue to grow.

- A dean always likes to be informed about any situation that is taking place in the dean's college or program or that involves the dean's staff or faculty. When the provost hands you a situation with a college, do not assume the provost will inform the dean. Informing the dean that you are involved in the situation is in your ballpark. Your communication with the dean can be done with an email; however, if you are new and in the process of building collegial relationships with the deans, meet in person.

- If you inform a dean about a particular situation that you are addressing and the dean says he or she will look into it, let that happen. Ask the dean how much time the dean needs and when you should reconnect. Let the dean know the time constraints given to you by the provost and then check back with the dean in a timely manner; understand that the dean may get busy and forget to get back with you.

Another political situation that might occur for you is one that happens between deans. Deans tend to be very protective of their people and their programs. Sometimes, little turf wars take place. When such a disturbance occurs, treading lightly might be the best action to take.

What might this look like when deans start a discussion about their turf? What should you do if you find yourself in the middle of their disagreement? And, more importantly, what do you do when the provost asks you to assist in finding a viable solution? This is where your knowledge of how deans interact with each other will be useful.

Most of the situations that arise between deans deal with course and program offerings or personnel issues. When new programs are approved, one dean might want the program in his or her college and another dean might think the program belongs in his or her own college. Several conversations will take place with the provost and, possibly, you, to help determine which college would be the best place for the new program.

Because they are professionals, the deans usually remain cordial with each other, especially in front of the provost. Don't let that play of agreement fool you. Deans are always eager to grow their colleges because, most of the time, having growth means that their personnel lines also increase. If you are invited by the provost to watch this process take place, be sure to make some mental notes about how the process works, what the deans share as reasons for the program to be in their own college, and how the provost makes the decision.

If the provost asks you to lead this particular type of meeting with two deans, here are a few things you can do to help find an appropriate decision that benefits both colleges and that satisfies both deans.

- Schedule an individual meeting with each dean.
- Ask the deans to provide support statements, explaining why the new program should be in their own college.
- Ask the deans to provide a degree plan for the new program. Each plan should detail the courses involved and the associated prerequisites. Creating such degree plans will take some time because faculty usually help to create degree plans.
- Determine what other colleges may be involved in the completion of the degree.
- Give the deans a deadline for completing the support statements. Deans are always busy, and having a deadline may help them stay focused.
- With your knowledge of the new program, do some research on where other universities have housed the same type of program.
- Develop a schematic of what the program would look like in each of the colleges. A degree plan could serve as a schematic.
- Meet with the provost and provide the provost with your findings. The provost will make the final decision.

While your position is that of a university administrator, deans hold academic positions and are also seen as administrators in their colleges. Helping deans as much as you can is also helping yourself in your position. Working with deans to garner a positive outcome for a situation, such as adding a new program, is most definitely a positive political move on your part.

DEPARTMENT POLITICS

The dean is seen as the political leader of his or her college, and there are definitely more politics at work within each college's various departments. Within the ranks of faculty, there is a definite hierarchy. Newly hired assistant professors, before they receive tenure, are considered junior faculty. When coming into a department, junior faculty often do not get their choice of offices. This may seem trite but, if an open office space happens to have an outside view, that office is considered prime real estate and usually will go to a senior faculty member.

Being a member of the junior faculty also means not always being offered course overloads, first authorships on research projects, or even an open office space. The low rank of junior faculty members is a political truth that you need to accept when you begin your academic life at a university. Such political truths affect your role as an associate provost in several ways.

In your role, this type of situation may never enter into your world. But you should be very aware of the political workings of an academic department, especially when the provost assigns you responsibilities in certain departments. Some faculty members hold more department power because of their years of service, grants they were awarded, or the number of research projects they have completed.

Sometimes the political nature of the department comes to light when a chairperson is being chosen. In some colleges, department chairpersons are permanently hired by the dean for that specific role. In other cases, department chairpersons are elected by the entire faculty or the position is assigned on a rotating basis. Junior faculty usually don't have the required tenure to serve in that capacity.

A department also has a life of its own. If there is any kind of disagreement within the ranks of the faculty members, you will most definitely feel it when you are called upon to address a situation.

Let's say a situation exists between a faculty member and the chairperson of the department and the provost asks you to determine what is actually taking place and to report back. After meeting with the chairperson of the department, you learn that, when the chairperson meets with the faculty member, their conversations have become very toxic and that the faculty member is "stirring up trouble" with other faculty members.

With this information in hand, you probably should meet with the faculty member and the chairperson individually to document their sides of the situation. Be prepared for the faculty member either refusing to meet with you because of your position or the faculty member making a request to have another person present during the meeting. If the faculty member decides he or she does not want to meet with you, tell the faculty member that is regrettable because you simply want to hear his or her side of the situation. If the faculty member requests that another person be present, agree. Having another person in the meeting will not change the conversation that has to take place.

When it comes to the conversation between you and the faculty member, a few questions should be asked. Your role in this situation is to gather information. Learn as much as you can about the faculty member before the meeting. How long has he or she been at the university? Has he or she served at other institutions? What does he or she teach? This is basic information.

- Inform the faculty member you will be taking note so you don't miss any important details.

- Ask the faculty member to describe department situations that are taking place. Such situations do not necessarily directly involve the faculty member.
- Begin discussing the problems at hand with lead questions, such as
- What do you see as the existing situation in the department?
- What kinds of behaviors have you noticed from those in the department?,
- What is your desired outcome from this situation?, or
- What types of actions could you take to improve the current situation?.
- When the conversation is over and before ending the meeting, be sure to ask the faculty member if there is anything else he or she wants to share.
- Make no promises. Just thank the faculty member for his or her time and say you will share all of the information with the provost.

After you meet with the faculty member, you will also have to meet with the chairperson of the department. The same steps and questions apply. The chairperson may also provide you with more definite descriptions of the behaviors of the faculty member. Sometimes faculty members leave out bits and pieces in the retelling of a situation. After you collect both sides of the story, so to speak, create a side-by-side chart of the information to correlate the information. This graphic might serve as part of a report you provide to the provost.

You might be thinking the most important issue here is finding a solution to the problem. However, in this particular situation, when you know you are in the middle of a potential political problem within the department, your most important consideration is how other faculty members view what is taking place and the possible actions you will take.

You represent the provost when trying to find a solution to this conflict. The provost usually does not interfere with department politics until a situation is brought to the provost's attention. Simply do what has previously been suggested. After collecting the needed information, complete a report for the provost and wait for further instructions.

Departmental politics are just as serious and important as any vote taking place on the floor of Congress. Keep this in mind when you become involved in a departmental situation. Be mindful that other faculty are watching how you handle yourself and address the situation. In fact, someone is always watching.

CULTURES AND TRADITIONS

If you have not had a chance to walk the campus, introduce yourself to other academics and faculty members, or even attend a sporting event, you might have limited knowledge about the existing culture of the institution. The culture of an institution is just as political as deciding on who to vote for in an election.

Years ago, a new high-school principal decided to end the age-old tradition of seniors driving around the campus on their last day of school. This tradition had been going on for many years. You could say it was part of the school's tradition. When the students and families found out the event had been canceled, they went straight to the superintendent with their complaints. Can you guess how the situation turned out?

If you think the seniors who washed their cars, filled them up with gas, and tested their car horns were going to be denied their rightful tradition and just walk away with smiles on their faces, oh, how wrong you would be. Regardless of the actual words that were spoken during the conversation between the principal and the superintendent, the students were allowed to make their traditional drive around the campus and the principal served for only one year at the high school.

What was the principal's crime? What wrong had he done? With his decision to cancel the senior drive around, he actually committed political suicide. The principal forgot that, to many, the traditions of a school are just as culturally important as its academics.

Your institution has the same kind of traditions and a cultural heritage. When you are appointed to the position of associate provost, do your due diligence to find out what those traditions are and their importance. Let's talk for a moment about the importance of these traditions and how you as an associate provost can play a part in them.

- Buy a lot of university t-shirts that have the institution's name and are in the school's colors. Wear these shirts to every sporting event you attend. Be sure to attend as many as you can and as often as you can.
- Buy professional clothing in your school's colors and wear these outfits to professional meetings and conferences. Also, be sure to wear your school colors when visiting other universities and colleges.
- Many universities have hand signals (appropriate hand signals), which are just as recognizable as a t-shirt or hat featuring the school's mascot. Learn what your institution's hand signal is (if it has one) and use it all the time.
- The university itself will have some particular traditions for its students. There might be a particular event that recognizes when juniors transition into their senior year. Freshman might be chosen as the ones to lead the football team out of the tunnel and onto the field. Respect these events and participate in them as often as possible.

How are buying a t-shirt and making hand signals seen as political actions? Who cares if you attend student functions? You are in administration. There are staff and faculty other than you to represent the university. The simple answer is that, anytime you can include yourself in the cultural activities of the university, don't think twice. Be there. You will definitely be adding to your currency as a political person on the campus.

POWER IN THE POSITION OR POSITION OF POWER

Many positions at a university come with an automatic understanding that power and authority are aligned to that position. Take, for instance, the presidency. The person who holds that position automatically has a line of power. His or her power is understood by and known to all faculty, academic unit heads, directors, staff members, vice presidents, provosts, and associate provosts—basically, everyone on the campus.

The president of the university may have power and authority over those at the university, but that power and authority are given to the president by the board of regents or the governing body of the university. Board members are usually appointed to their positions by a governor (at least that is how it is done in several states). Board members have some kind of affiliation with the university; most are alumni. Board members automatically possess power and authority over the workings of the university.

How might their authority come into play? Is their authority automatically assumed? Does their power mean they can micromanage day-to-day operations? Yes and no.

For instance, a dean recommends that a person be hired. That request goes to the provost. The provost presents that request (and others) to the president. The president then presents all personnel requests to the board of regents. The board, not the dean, the provost, or the president, hires that person. These administrators only make recommendations. Only the board has the power and authority to hire personnel.

Usually, your contact with the board of regents will take place during regularly scheduled board meetings. At many universities, board meetings take place four times per year on a regularly scheduled meeting date. During your tenure as an associate provost, you may come in direct contact with board members. Your conversation may be about the weather or your family. In some cases, a board member might be fishing for some information you have about a particular situation taking place at the university. A board member might ask how the new provost is working out or whether any faculty situations are taking place.

Why should you be attentive to a conversation with a board member? Aren't the board members nice people? Don't they have the best interests of the university at heart? Of course, they are and they do. However, sometimes a board member might want information that exceeds his or her role. In that case, remember a board member's authority and power exist when the board is convened as the board. The person you meet at Walmart asking these questions as a single individual has really no power.

But there you stand in the middle of Walmart being asked questions that you know you shouldn't answer. You know about confidentiality and the power the board as a whole has. How do you respond? What can you say that will comply with confidentiality requirements and still respect the position of the board member?

In your kindest and most congenial voice, tell the board member that you have not been involved in the situation he or she is referring to. Inform the board member that you would be happy to take any questions to the provost. The provost can then forward the board member's questions or concerns to the president, and the president will be happy to respond to the board member.

Talk about the weather. Ask how the kids are. Keep the conversations friendly and simple and as short as you can. Share some of the great and wonderful things taking place on the campus. As soon as you end the conversation, inform the provost about this encounter, identifying the board member and relating what was discussed. Rest assured that the provost will inform the president.

In the position of associate provost, you do hold some power and authority. That particular power comes from your position, but the authority you have comes only from the provost. It will serve you well to learn this difference. Unfortunately, some administrators have never learned the difference. While you are contemplating your own position of power and authority, you should recognize several other staff members on the campus as people who hold different positions of power.

- **Administrative assistants**: Regardless of the department, administrative assistants can and will make your life easier. There is an old saying in the field of prekindergarten through twelfth-grade education. The person who really runs the school is the school secretary, not the principal. This is the real truth! While the position of administrative assistant does not carry much authority, administrative assistants do have a great deal of power. Be sure to recognize them as valuable members of the institution.
- **Custodial staff**: These people can make your office and even your building a show place. They are often forgotten because they are not always visible when daily operations are taking place. Make sure you

recognize their efforts. In most cases, they are very proud of their contributions to keeping their buildings pristine as well as to keeping the university, as a whole, looking its best.

- **Police department**: Make sure to play nice with these folks. When you lock your keys in the car, and you know this might happen, they will come to your aid. They will even come to help you if you have a dead battery. Even more importantly, the police department restores order when chaos develops on campus.
- **Technology department**: Sometimes these folks are forgotten because the technology at the university and in your office is working. When technology hits a snag or quits working, these technicians become the most important people on the campus, maybe even on the planet.
- **Academic advisors**: Each department has a set of professional advisors or uses faculty advisors. These people help students complete a degree plan. Their goal is to use a degree plan to inform students about what courses they need so that students do not need to repeat courses or take unnecessary courses. They are essential to the academic working of a department.

These are only a few of the people on the campus that hold positions of power without having actual lines of authority. While they are not the president or an associate provost, they have a great deal of power, especially when they are needed.

UNSPOKEN AUTHORITY

In most institutions, another group has some level of unspoken authority: the alumni. Members of this group, more than any other, hold the traditions of the institution near and dear to their hearts. They may not work at or attend the university but never dismiss their authority.

Members of this particular group have historical knowledge of the university and want their children, grandchildren, neighbors, friends, and even the strangers they meet to attend "their alma mater." These men and women have community connections, they know members of the board of regents, and their influence reaches wide proportions.

Alumni possess a great deal of cultural currency. Take every opportunity to get to know these folks. Attend alumni functions. Network with them as much as you can because they might serve as conduits between some of your students and their possible future professions. If the members of this group do not work at or attend the university, how might you, as the associate provost, become associated with members of the group?

Well, here's what might take place. The president gets a phone call from an alumni member asking for a favor. The alumni member is requesting that his granddaughter be housed in a particular dorm because that's where all of her high-school friends will be living. Unfortunately, that residence hall is full. The alumni member asks if the president can do anything to help his granddaughter.

The president turns the request over to the provost. The provost then turns the request over to you and asks that you look into the situation to find out what can be done. When the request comes in, the provost also informs you that the person making the request is an alumni member. Without saying "make this happen," the provost is really saying, "Do whatever you have to do to get the granddaughter in the requested dorm." Does this request equate to favoritism? Sometimes. Does this request equate to special treatment for some and not others? Sometimes. Should you learn to play this game? Most definitely.

When you get this request, everything on your to-do list disappears. Every meeting you have scheduled has to be rescheduled. The most important task you have to address on this particular day is the request from the provost. Remember who really sent that request. That's right, the president.

As with other situations that have been put in your hands, let's arrange a plan of action for you.

- Ask the provost for as much information as possible: the student's name, the dorm requested, the alumni member's name.
- When you have the name of the student and the requested dorm, start your problem-solving process.
- Contact the director of the residential life department and fill him in on the request, emphasizing the alumni-to-president path of the request.
- If the director informs you that the requested dorm is full and there is already a waiting list, continue the conversation with, "OK. Let's think of some way we can make this request happen."
- If the director informs you that the open time for room changes will take place in a day or two, you automatically reserve one of the rooms that opens up in the alumni member's granddaughter's name.
- In the meantime, while waiting for another plan of action or the day when room change requests are made, ask the director to review previous room change requests to determine if, by moving others around, the alumni's granddaughter can be moved into the requested dorm.
- Keep the provost informed at every juncture so the provost can keep the president informed.

- Continue working with the director until the problem is resolved. This may take a couple of days, but do not put this situation on a back burner. Find a workable solution.

Because you are a forward-thinking associate provost, you might be wondering why the president or the provost didn't just make the call to the director of the residential life department? Why was this task given to you?

The provost or the president could call that director and make the request, and it would be done. However, this action may well cause some bad feelings with those in the residential life department because they have already had to turn down requests made by other students and parents. Finding another way to address the situation and use existing university practices is the best way to help the president help the alumni member and, in turn, show them you are dependable.

As you serve in the role of associate provost and move in and out of administrative meetings and happenings, you will begin to notice how busy and hectic the world of administration really is. This serves as the reason for you being called in to assist with many situations that arise. Anything you can do or any service you can provide to ease the workload of the provost and especially of the president will not go unnoticed.

When might it be appropriate to use your position? Should you introduce yourself as Dr. Wonderful, the new associate provost, and wait for the adulation to begin? Should people bow their heads in awe when you are seen walking across the campus? Don't even think about it.

Be wise enough to use your position to help you solve problems, address student concerns, and work with others to build lasting collegial relationships. People who hold positions of authority and power, even you, should never flaunt them. Always treat people with respect and dignity, no matter what position they hold.

CHAIN OF COMMAND

Previously, you have been reminded about the importance of confidentiality, assumed and unspoken authority, and positions of power. The role of deans and departmental politics have also been discussed. What might have been left out is the importance of following the chain of command.

This might be a good point to discuss the importance of following the chain of command, especially at an institution of higher education. You most often find the importance of following the chain of command when dealing with departmental situations, especially when the dean and a faculty member are at the heart of that situation.

Here's another "what if" exercise for you to practice. A faculty member asks to visit with you about a problem he is having with another person in his department. He has brought the situation to the dean, and nothing has been done to relieve the problem. So, the faculty member has come to you to get some help.

After hearing what is taking place in the department between the two faculty members, there are definitely some questions that need to be asked before taking any steps.

- "What did the dean say when you talked with her?"
- "Have you tried to talk with the other faculty member to try to get a solution?"
- "What expectations do you have for a resolution?"
- "What actions do you want me to take?"

Before the conversation ends, you need to inform the faculty member that, until you are directed by the provost to step in, the dean is the one who will be responsible for the solution.

You might be thinking that your responses go against your attempts to build collegial relationships, especially with faculty members. However, you are also trying to build collegial relationships with the deans. In this case, the chain of commands trumps all.

There's another piece of advice that is relevant to pass on at this time. As harsh and direct as it may seem, if you start to involve yourself with the day-to-day operations that take place in departments, you will have no time to take care of anything else, including the responsibilities assigned to you. If faculty start looking to you to solve certain situations for them, you will circumvent the power and authority of the dean. Never a good idea.

In you're working with other administrators, especially vice presidents, the same consideration of chain of command is in play. Pull out that organizational chart once again and locate your place on the chart. You answer to any and every person holding a position that is above yours. You should adhere to the chain-of-command rule.

If a situation arises with a faculty member and you are fully aware of the importance of honoring the chain of command when dealing with such issues, you should probably follow a previously discussed process that has been successful in the past. The process includes

- gathering as much information as you can (you already know to do this),
- informing the dean of the college that you will be having a conversation with one of his or her faculty members,
- collecting information from the meeting with the faculty member,

- reporting your findings to the dean, and
- completing a summary report for the provost.

Does this sound familiar? Of course, it does. Hopefully, this is the process that you will burn into your memory when the provost asks you to investigate any situation: Find out what is taking place; find out who ALL the players are; take copious notes; remember to follow the chain of command; and always keep the provost informed. The provost may not always ask for information on some of your accomplished tasks; nonetheless, have your collected data ready in case the provost has any questions.

As you stood in line waiting for your turn on the roller coaster, you watched every dip and curve the tram took. You listened to screaming riders as they were thrown about.

Never in your wildest imagination did you think a ride on a roller coaster would one day mirror your life in the world of higher education politics.

LET'S LOOK BACK

Following are some reminders about campus politics and positions, things to keep in mind as you begin your tenure as an associate provost:

- You may not like the person who holds a position of authority but you must respect the position. Even if the person that you don't like is the president of the university, that person still holds a position of authority. Your personal feelings are secondary to your ability to work with, beside, and for a person you don't like unless you have another administrative job in the wings. So, as it is sometimes said, "Suck it up, buttercup."
- No matter how trivial you think a piece of information might be, if it pertains to the university and its workings, always tell your immediate supervisor, the provost. You will need to walk a fine line in distinguishing between what is necessary to share and what is gossip.
- Pay close attention to those people on campus who may not hold positions of power but who always exhibit a sense of authority because of where they work or the job they do.
- Political plays that take place on the campus usually stem from those in power, those who want power, and those who believe they are in power. Learn who these people are and do not play games with them. They usually have personal agendas that will and can interfere with your role as an associate provost.

Are you feeling a little queasy as you learn about the ups and downs that can take place when university politics come into play? Do you feel a scream about to rip from your mouth as you go into the twists and turns of that roller coaster ride called campus politics? Of course, you do. Being a part of the political workings at a university may seem a little messy until you learn who actually holds real positions of power. Once you learn how things really work, the road through political situations will become much easier.

Such is the life of an associate provost trying to learn the path that the art of politics takes in the day-to-day operations of a university. After a few twists and turns, you'll learn the ins and outs of the politics that could affect or influence you as an associate provost. Here are some words of advice: Learn quickly.

LET'S TALK ABOUT THE REAL WORLD

The most important, last bit of advice you should keep in your memory bank regarding university politics is the fact that university politics are real. Whether the political interplay is out in the open or stands as a known undercurrent of operations in academics, there are certain players and rules you should know.

The person that you will work with the most and on almost a daily basis is the provost.

Hopefully, the provost will help to guide you through some of the politics taking place at the university. This doesn't mean you should hide your head in the sand or run away from potentially difficult situations if they have a political overtone.

You will be asked for favors and special considerations by staff and faculty across various campus departments. People will expect you to share information that is privileged or confidential. Faculty members will seek you out to solve problems for them without talking to their dean or the provost. These political plays will take up a lot of your time if you let them. So, don't let them.

As a newly appointed associate provost, you will become aware of the political interplay that take place in your administrative area, in your interactions with staff and faculty, and in the university as a community. You must learn by doing and, unfortunately, sometimes by making mistakes. In the real world of university politics, it is always best to keep some opinions to yourself, to never forget who you are talking to, and to treat the custodian with the same respect you give the president of the university.

WHAT WOULD YOU DO?

Learning about the political workings of a university might take you a little time because some of the events that are political in nature don't always happen in a timely manner. The scenario below illustrates a possible situation that could occur in relation to your early actions as a savvy politically aware associate provost. Possible actions have been provided and are listed in no particular order.

A scheduled board of regents meeting is taking place in a few days and you find out you are expected to attend the meeting. You know the provost has been working with other administrators and the president in preparation for the meeting. When you arrive at the meeting, you see name cards in front of certain chairs but no name card for you. Luckily, you find an empty chair behind where the provost will be sitting. When people start coming in for the meeting, another university administrator walks up to you and says you are in his seat and asks you to move.

From the following list of possible actions to take, knowing you are in a very political setting and are new to your position, what might you do?

- __ Move without saying a word.
- __ Apologize for sitting in the wrong place.
- __ Ask the provost's administrative assistant to make the chair closest to the provost your permanent place to sit during board meetings and to create a name card for you.
- __ Stay where you are and remind the other administrator that there are other chairs available.
- __ Stay where you are and let the other administrator know you are strategically sitting close to the provost in case the provost needs you to check on something.

Chapter 5

Let's Go to the Midway (Having Fun as an Associate Provost)

The previous chapters examine the role of the associate provost in light of the responsibilities and tasks connected to the position and provide countless suggestions and recommendations for how to make the position your very own. Some of the tasks and responsibilities seem daunting—doable only by someone who has special powers and wears a flowing red cape with the letter "S" on the front. With that said, an associate provost can have fun. Let's continue with our trip to the Texas State Fair, and let's play some games.

Fairs always feature, in addition to wonderful food choices and interesting exhibits, some games. When you first see the Midway, as it is referred to at the State Fair of Texas, you are drawn in by the music, games, and the stuffed animals. You just know you will be carrying home one of those stuffed giraffes before the day is done. What you might not realize at this time is that the games are not always as easy as you think.

For instance, you step up to the basketball throw with the knowledge that you were the MVP at the last YMCA basketball tournament. You're feeling pretty confident about your basketball skills. However, no one tells you that the basketballs are a little deflated and the rim is a little smaller than regulation size. If you knew this information before you started playing this game you would realize, "you ain't never gonna make a basket."

OK, so maybe the basketball toss is not your game today.

Moving on down the Midway, you see the milk bottle game. The objective is to throw a baseball at a stack of wooden milk bottles and knock them over. Not only are you good at basketball, you were also a star pitcher on the school's softball team. You've got this! In your hands, you have the balls ready to throw. You wind up for the first throw, let the ball fly, and not one milk bottle falls down. You throw a second and third time, and nothing happens. How can this be? What you might not know is that the bottom of the milk bottles are weighted down and not even Babe Ruth could knock them down.

Looking around the Midway, you don't really see many stuffed animals heading home with winners and you may deduce that the games are not in your favor. Why, then, go to the Midway? Because it's fun. There is loud music playing. Bells and whistles are going off around all of the rides, and there are screams of laughter coming from every direction. You can hardly wait to get to the Midway.

As an associate provost, you will have many days that are hectic and even some when you want to pull your hair out. First, don't pull your hair out. Some of those first crazy days when you are learning the ropes will provide some wonderful and fun times to look forward to—much like your visit to the Midway.

WHEN PARENTS VISIT

Most universities and colleges offer parents the opportunity to explore the campus where they are sending their child. These "parents' weekends" are always so much fun and they provide you with a chance to meet and talk to parents about the wonderful academic programs offered by your university. During parents' weekend, students usually move through a prearranged schedule and parents also have a chance to learn more about the university through various meetings they can attend.

Parents are always excited about these visits because they believe that, in attending college, their child is taking steps to move forward in his or her life. The campus usually looks wonderful. Buildings have been cleaned to a bright shine. Everyone they meet is kind and helpful. And your presence at this event provides you with an opportunity to shine as an ambassador of knowledge about the university and its workings.

In some cases, you might be asked to address a group of parents. If you speak to parents, you should share with them the following facts about the university:

- The university will treat their student as an adult.
- Correspondence from the university will always go to their student, not to them.
- Parking tickets are issued to the owner of the car, which might be the parents. When a student has accumulated a certain number of tickets, the car—the car that is owned by the parents—will be towed.
- Students live in the dorms; parents don't. Whatever happens in a dorm falls on the student's shoulders.

- Any disciplinary action that is taken against a student is a direct result of the student's actions, not the actions of the student's parents.
- Students are responsible for meeting all deadlines imposed by the university, including those for advising requirements, those for applying for graduation, and those for paying tuition.
- Their students will have many academic choices to make: whether to attend class, which courses to take, whether to study for an upcoming event, whether to meet program deadlines. Parents don't make these decisions; their child does.
- If a student violates the code of conduct at the university, consequences will ensue and can be very severe.

Of course, you will deliver these messages and more with some humor and straightforward talk. Parents will appreciate truthfulness and honesty. Many of the parents will actually be glad to know that the university is helping them help their students become functioning adults, at least while they are at the university. Be prepared for some parents who have been helicopter parents to stay in that role.

During parents' weekend, if you meet with parents one-on-one, be sure to ask about the field of study their child has decided upon. Hand out your business cards and ask them to contact you if any questions or concerns come up. Speak highly of the campus offices that stand ready to assist their child with housing or financial-aid issues. You might even consider giving the parents a quick campus tour, showing them some of the main buildings, such as the library or the bookstore. These actions go a long way in building relationships with parents.

In some instances, the provost might call upon you to meet with a special parent. This could be a VIP, an alumni family, or a friend of the president. Whatever the case might be, always showcase the university. You might take this parent to the newest building on campus. You might direct this parent's path to the recreation center or library. Find out what program this parent's child is considering and be sure to tour that department together.

You should always attend meetings with the parents of future students of your institution. Your willingness to help and be a part of the process will bring you a lot of fun. Now, will it be as much fun as playing a game on the Midway? It may be. Will there be a stuffed animal waiting for you at the end of the weekend? There probably will not be. In this short time with parents, you have already started the process of building lasting relationships.

CAMPUS EVENTS

Besides hosting parents' weekends, colleges and universities always have something going on besides students attending classes. Various programs at the university may invite guests to visit the campus for special events. Something is always happening in the athletic department. Student groups are often invited to campus for tours. In the summer, all kinds of student camps are taking place. You can have a great deal of fun being a part of these days.

The university is the best place to enjoy having students everywhere. Cheerleader camps bring bright and enthusiastic students to campus. Band camps also bring life to various parts of the campus. And what comes with students? That's right, their parents. These events provide you with more opportunities to give parents a sales pitch for attending your university. They can be seen as almost a captive audience, just waiting for you to show them the campus and its wonders.

Not all the events on the campus involve parents. There are symposiums, guest lectures, musical performances, and theatrical presentations, not to mention various athletic games. If your day is filled with obstacles and you need to lift your spirits, attend a musical performance. If you need to find some fun, attend a basketball game. There is no possible way you won't enjoy these two campus happenings.

Most of the events that take place on the campus have usually taken place there before. Departments know how to plan for their special events. Athletic competitions have been scheduled in advance for months. However, what if your institution is hosting an on-campus event for a new student group and the provost has called on you to lead this effort? What are the steps you would take to make the event a success?

After meeting with the provost to get the provost's directions and a list of goals to accomplish, consider taking the following steps:

- Identify the contact person from among the event organizers.
- Contact the contact person to determine the dates of the event, the amount and type of space the event needs, and an estimate of how many people will be visiting the campus for this event.
- Once the dates for the event are determined and you know the amount and type of space that is needed, begin discussions with the university side of the house to locate the needed space.
- Begin asking for campus volunteers, especially from the offices that focus on student involvement, to help coordinate the event.
- If you have enough time before the event date, invite community members and other administrators to attend the event.

- Notify the university's parking department early enough to inform officers about visitors coming onto campus for the event and to determine whether parking passes will be needed.
- Talk with the food services department to inform its director about visitors coming onto campus for the event and to discuss whether refreshments or lunches might be needed.
- Since the visitors on the campus will probably include minors, be sure to have a police presence available for the event.
- Stay in contact with the event organizers to be aware of any changes that need to be made.
- When event participants arrive on campus, be there, if possible, to greet them.
- When the event is over, send a thank-you note to the contact person.
- When the event is over, send a thank-you note to all internal entities that helped make the day a success.
- Provide a summary of the event to the provost. The provost may direct you to provide the same documentation to the university's communications department in order to give credit to the university for hosting the event.

With your schedule and the many tasks you are responsible for, you may not have time to attend many events. In addition, the provost may never call on you to arrange such an event. However, if the provost does ask that you do so, you'll be ready. Do what you can to make this a landmark event on your campus.

Attending campus events, regardless of the type, can bring a little laughter and lightness into your associate provost world. Attending these events should also provide you with a sense of pride in your institution and its people. Pay attention to the university's calendar of events. This will help you know what's taking place on the campus and how many events you can actually attend.

MEMORABLE TIMES WITH STUDENTS

You may encounter many challenging situations involving students and their academic needs. Most of the student situations that come to your desk center around problems and difficulties. You usually have to run interference with other academics on behalf of students or try to keep a student from jumping off a ledge. Nonetheless, there are also times when working with students is very rewarding, times when working with and helping students will bring a smile to your face.

Part of your work with students will be to help students through the completion of their degrees. Students may need help with an advising issue or help with getting the classes they need. Once you assist a student, you may never know what happens in their future academic lives. However, sometimes you do.

Ready for a practice exercise? Sure, you are. A student visits your office and needs some help in completing her degree. The student has completed 190 credit hours but has not earned a degree—that's right, no degree. The student also shares that she have been denied additional financial aid because of her current grade point average. She has no idea what to do from this point and has come to you for any kind of assistance. So, without having a magic wand to take away some of the credit hours and to reinstate some financial aid, what exactly can you do?

You can:

- locate the student's transcript.
  - Why? To gain information about the student's academic record. Has the student changed her major? Has the student had to repeat courses? What's the student's grade point average in her program of study?
- ask an academic advisor to complete a degree audit.
  - Why? To determine how many credit hours taken actually relate to the student's degree plan and what courses might be missing.
- contact the director of the office of financial aid to determine what can be done to reinstate the student's financial aid.
  - Why? Because the director of the office is the only one at this point that can find a way to reinstate the financial aid or to determine if additional funds are available.
- contact the director for the general studies degree (sometimes called interdisciplinary studies) and ask for his or her advice.

  - Why? With all of the credit hours accumulated by the student, there may be a way to craft a general studies degree from the courses the student has passed.

While these steps will help you help the student, the best outcome is to provide a student with a pathway to completing his or her degree and, hopefully, with some kind of financial aid. Requesting help from the right people in the right places helps you make students' academic lives a bit easier. Chalk up the days when you are able to solve a problem for a student as ones that bring smiles to everyone's faces.

One of the most important and joyous times you can have with students is their graduation day. Whether graduation takes place on the campus or at another site, all you will see for miles and miles are smiling parents, grand-parents, and visitors. Deans, faculty members, and university administrators are decked out in flowing robes with brightly colored hoods. Happy family members are ready to see their students walk across the stage and graduate.

As an administrator for the university, you may be called upon to sit on the stage and greet each student with a congratulatory comment and a handshake. As you begin shaking hands with students, you may recognize some of them as students you were instrumental in helping earn their degree. You may not have heard from students after they left your office, but there they are walking the stage. Air horns going off, parents' yells, and even a few whistles being blown makes this a special time.

Because the position of associate provost is an administrative position at the university, you may be invited to join student groups and take part in their activities. Most of these gatherings, such as culinary program offerings and opportunities from educational courses, will be academic in nature. These opportunities to be with students in their academic habitats allow you to con-nect with them. The relationships you build with students on the campus can be lasting ones. Don't miss too many chances to work with students and to take part in their campus lives.

A semester before high-school students graduate, they apply for as many scholarships as they can. If they want to attend your institution, they apply for and, many times, are awarded scholarships based on meeting certain criteria. When it's time to make the announcements for the scholarship recipients, be sure to sign up for that duty. That day will be a memorable one.

If you are the person assigned to hand out the scholarship letters to high-school students, handing them out will be memorable because you might be the first person from the university with whom they actually have contact and you are handing out money! You will definitely be remembered. Parents and family members will want to shake your hand. Their words of thanks are heartfelt. The excitement stems not only from the sheer joy of graduating from high school but also from receiving a monetary scholarship to attend your university.

The times and events that revolve around students on campus and those who are potential students will help to revive your spirit on a challenging day, give you a place to be away from the stack of work that is sitting on your desk, and a way to put turbulent situations with faculty on back burners.

If you are asked to serve on a scholarship committee, sign up. Such service provides great possibilities for working with internal and external entities. School counselors are always involved. Families are eager to be a part of the process that might open a door for their child to go to college. The univer-sity is ready to add another student to the academic population. Scholarship processes are something that you should be familiar with, since both internal and external entities are involved and giving away university money is always fun.

What are some of the things you should know about the scholarship process?

- Be familiar with the scholarship guidelines (time frames, requirements).
- Determine the prerequisites for scholarships.
- Determine the amounts dedicated to each scholarship.
- Work with departments to get information about specialized scholarships.
- Visit with high-school counselors to talk about scholarships offered from the university.
- Be part of the awards process when decisions are made.

How does working with a scholarship committee translate into a fun time with students? Giving away money should always be fun. More importantly, for you as an academic, making sure another student can receive some assistance that will allow the student to earn a college degree, not to mention the smiles on the faces of the student and the student's family when the announcements is made, should put you on cloud nine.

FUN TIMES WITH THE PROVOST

You might be thinking that the provost will need you only to address campus problems or difficult situations. These are not the only times you will be needed. As you become aware of how the provost likes to operate, there are times when it can be fun to work beside them. This could be in a meeting or at an event or even in one-on-one conversations.

The size of your institution and the number of other associate provosts that are on your campus determine how much individual time you have with the provost. Most of the time you work within the authority of their position. You represent the provost and the university every day; however, there are times to have fun and really enjoy your working assignments.

- During some lunch meetings, the provost will recognize some of the attendees as people he or she may not want to sit next to. Maybe the provost has had some unpleasant words with the other attendee. Maybe the provost actually doesn't like the other person. So, instead of sitting at a table with other university administrators, the provost might direct you to sit at the table with that attendee. Don't be surprised when you look at the provost and he or she is grinning from ear to ear.

- Don't be surprised if the provost gives you an unexpected duty here and there. One of those duties might be to take the provost's place at a speaking engagement. For instance, let's say the provost was supposed to be the spokesperson at an awards ceremony to recognize faculty members for their years of service. Minutes before the ceremony is to begin, the provost informs you that because he or she is receiving an award, you will be serving as the master of ceremonies. Again, don't be surprised if you look at the provost and he or she is grinning from ear to ear.
- When the provost is in an embarrassing situation, you may be called upon to help. Pretend you are at a party of some kind, talking with the provost, when a person, let's say, a scantily dressed person, approaches you. You can tell the provost is a little uncomfortable with the situation. Suddenly, the provost makes excuses and exits the conversation, leaving you with the scantily dressed person. As you try to focus your gaze elsewhere, you might happen to notice a grinning provost.

It might take you a little while to learn when the provost is joking. As you begin your tenure with the provost, there are times when you will be able to joke with the provost. After you work with the provost for a while, you will come to know how much he or she relies on you and your leadership abilities. There will be many more times when you and the provost will share happy events that take place at the university or applaud accomplishments of others. When these kinds of moments come your way, have fun!

ATTENDING CONFERENCES

One of the best times you will have, when serving as an associate provost, is the travel that is required for your position. The conference hotels are usually very nice. You have a per diem allowance for food and in-city transportation, and there are always things to see and do when visiting from out of town. Of course, you do have to attend the conference, which, after all, is the reason for the trip.

Not only do presentations at conferences add to your knowledge about issues in higher education, they allow you to network with other administrators. The contacts you make at many conferences could possibly lead to other employment opportunities if the need arises as well as to consulting and research possibilities. There are also vendors that have free giveaways; all you have to do is talk to them for a few minutes, and you walk away with some pens, notepads, and several other trinkets.

Traveling with colleagues also provides you with opportunities to become more familiar with coworkers and other academics. You are away from the university, and the goal, after attending all the conference sessions, is to not talk about school or current situations. This should be a time when you can relax, get to know others on a personal basis, and have some fun. See the city sights, visit museums, take in a show. You will be back on the campus soon enough, and that real world of university life isn't going away. Attending a conference might be just what you need to unwind and take a breather from all of your duties.

LET'S LOOK BACK

Having fun on the Midway at the State Fair of Texas is a given. Even though some of the games favor the barkers and vendors, it's still fun, and, occasionally, you do win a stuffed giraffe. You as an associate provost will have to find your own kind of fun and enjoyment. You might enjoy helping potential students and their parents find the library or introducing them to professors and the dean of the relevant college.

Joy and fun might present themselves when you attend a campus event or you are the catalyst a student needs to be able to attend your university. Working closely with the provost will help to create a positive working relationship that will help to smooth some of the difficult times. Not everything about your position and duties will be daunting and bothersome. With all of the situations that you will deal with on a regular basis, some being very difficult, have a little fun when you can.

LET'S TALK ABOUT THE REAL WORLD

The position of associate provost usually is not associated with having fun. Difficult situations, unhappy people, and student crises are often what you might face on any given day. Eight-hour days can oftentimes turn into ten- or twelve-hour days. There are very few days when you can "skip school" and hide. Your life as an associate provost and the work assigned to you requires a lot of time and effort.

If you don't have a fair in town and can't get away to visit the State Fair of Texas, you are going to have to find some fun elsewhere. Take advantage of campus events that renew your reasons for being an educator and for being in higher education. While there may not be many games to play or rides to ride, you can still bring some joy to whatever you do.

WHAT WOULD YOU DO?

You will not have a problem staying busy in your role as an associate provost. On most days, you won't have to worry about where your day is going or about a leftover concern from the previous day that has to be addressed. Your calendar will do all the talking for you. So, with the many situations coming your way, how do you find time for a few actions that will bring some smiles into your day? The scenario below sounds very simplistic. Choices have to be made in order for you to fulfill your associate provost duties as well as bring a little bit of fun into your world. The action statements are in no particular order.

You have had a pretty tough week. You need to investigate and complete a report about a project assigned to you by the provost within a few days. The director in one of your departments just put in his resignation. Two angry parents have called the president because their students are having problems in some of their classes. And you have averaged three meetings per day. It's been a very busy and hectic week.

After looking at the university calendar, you see that high-school students are on campus, participating in a band camp activity; the agriculture department is hosting a Future Farmers of America conference; a musical is being offered by the fine arts department; and the culinary cafe student program is offering lunch on campus. Opportunities to have fun abound.

So, what's the problem? You are looking for things to do on campus to lift your spirits. You are looking for things that will bring a smile to your face and put a little joy in your life. The jobs on your desk are not going anywhere. The situations that occur are still going to be situations in the morning. The problem centers on what to do and how much to do to renew and lift your spirits. The dilemma is not really a problem, just a time-management issue, right? All you want to do is have a little fun.

Here are a few considerations if you want to take a day off and still stay on campus.

- __ Inform your administrative assistant that you will be out of the office and on campus for the day and that you will have your phone, in case any emergency should arise.
- __ Determine the time frames for each of the campus events.
- __ Arrange a schedule that allows you to attend as many of the on-campus functions as possible.
- __ Periodically check in with your administrative assistant.

- __ Introduce yourself to as many visitors and family members as possible. Be sure to carry as many business cards as possible and readily hand them out.
- __ Complete a report for the provost about your day of "fun" and all the contacts that you made.

This scenario is a little different from the others presented in previous and future chapters. There is no real pressing problem that needs a solution. No one is waiting for you at a meeting, and no reports are on fire. The only thing that is needed is for you to take a break, have a little fun, and enjoy the events that are taking place on the campus. You really don't need to make a schedule or have many action statements. All you really need is to have a little joy. Let your campus happenings help you find that joy.

Chapter 6

Fried Butter and More (Making Tough Decisions)

Going to the State Fair of Texas and choosing what food to buy is nothing like going to McDonald's and choosing between a quarter pounder and a fish sandwich. There are the standard options, such as corny dogs, corn on the cob dipped in melted butter, and cotton candy. Choosing among only three kinds of food is easy. However, the food offerings at the fair cover a wide range of choices.

While it was never easy to make food choices, choosing foods at the State Fair became a little harder because of Abel Gonzalez, Jr. In 2006, Abel Gonzalez, Jr., brought a new concoction to the Big Tex Choice Awards Food Competition: fried coke (Grossman, n.d.). That's when it became even harder to make a decision about to eat at the fair.

As soon as you hit the grounds of the fair, smells literally attack your nasal passages. Just as you do at any restaurant, you have to make some choices. These food choices are not like choosing whether to go to the Midway or the automobile building first. These food choices are a little harder to make because everything smells and looks so good. Some of the food choices are so unusual, they cannot be found in area restaurants.

So, imagine yourself standing in the middle of the food court at the fair. Down one row of the food court, you have choices such as Fried Soul Food egg rolls, Dim Sim Loco burritos, and deep-fried "country cookouts." On the other side of the food court, you can choose to have a "Motherclucker" chicken sandwich, a Cajun lobster bisque croquette, or a "Fat Elvis" (bigtex. com/plan-your-visit/food/new food/, n.d.).

The fair comes to town only one time per year, and so do these food choices. What should you do to take advantage of all these choices? Should you start on one side of the food court and work your way down to each food booth, sampling a little as you go? Should you do that before you go to the

Midway? Or should you visit a few exhibits, come back to the food court, visit the other side of the food court, and end up with a "Fat Elvis"?

There are too many foods to choose from and only one day to visit the fair. So many things to see, so many games to play, and so many rides to ride. Do you have a plan in place to help you make your choices? Do you have a dietary concern that would prevent you from eating a "Motherclucker" chicken sandwich? Do you have enough time to try a little bit of everything?

When at the fair, you have to forget your diet, throw out any beliefs about what fried foods do to your cholesterol levels, and never worry about the caloric content of anything you are going to eat. For a few hours, it just doesn't matter. With so many choices, what's the real dilemma? If you are hungry for a taco, just find the taco stand. If you want something really sweet, go ahead and buy a fried Twinkie. If you've never had a deep-fried "country cookout," have one. You won't find one of those in a drive-thru at McDonald's.

Most won't consider choosing food at the fair to be a hard decision to make—it's kind of simple, really. Just choose the one you want and enjoy. Regardless of the decision process you use to choose between buying a corny dog or a Dim Sim Loco burrito, you still have to make a decision.

Now think about this for a minute. You used your sense of smell to lead you to the food court. You bought extra tickets just in case you wanted to try two or three different foods. You looked at the number of people standing in line at each of the food booths before making your final choice. You actually made several decisions before you had even taken one bite of.

It would be so easy to tell you that the decisions you will have to make as an associate provost will be just as easy as deciding what to eat while visiting the fair. Wouldn't it be nice to believe that every decision you make will be met with total agreement and resounding applause? Oh, well, that would be nice.

DECISION-MAKING 101

Whether you are at a fair or working as an associate provost, there are some basics for making decisions. However, you need to have a clear understanding that making food choices at the fair is a tad bit easier than making choices in the university setting, choices that will affect the institution and its people.

Even though you are probably pretty handy at making decisions by now, let's start with some basic ground rules for making decisions at your new level. Regardless of whether the situation involves a student, a parent, a faculty member, or a university situation, you should use the following steps:

- Gather as much information as possible during the beginning phase of a decision-making process. Be prepared for this step to be time consuming.
- When you start gathering information, people tend to tell you "a bunch of stuff." Some of that "stuff" is not necessary. Try your best to keep people on topic.
- Check and recheck the information you gather for accuracy. This means talking to as many people as you can that are involved in the situation and determining the common threads that are present in every piece of collected information.
- Determine what you really need to know. Review the decision that needs to be made. For instance, if the decision you have to make revolves around a grade for a student, don't worry about the student's parking tickets.
- Create a list of tasks that need to be done as you prepare to make a final decision. Making decisions at your level usually has time constraints.
- Determine the best way to address the situation. You've talked to those involved in the situation. You've collected a great deal of valuable information. You are ready to make a decision. Is an email an appropriate way to deliver your findings and, possibly, your decision? Did the provost ask you to send your findings to him or her before talking to others? Should you have a face-to-face meeting with those involved?
- **ALWAYS** check university policies. Many times you will be able to let policies do your talking as well as guide your decision-making.
- **ALWAYS** keep the provost informed of the actions you plan to take. If the provost has given you a problem to solve that needs a decision, regardless of the level of difficulty, always inform the provost about the actions you will be taking. Also, consider sending the provost a synopsis of the information you have gathered, the people you have talked to, and the plans you are going to follow when making the decision.

Remember that the provost has complete authority over YOUR decision-making process. You may work with a provost who just wants to be informed of your final decision. You have the full and complete support of this type of provost. They trust your decision-making skills because you have previously made good decisions that were beneficial to the university and the academic community.

Or you may work for a provost that wants you to check in at each step of the decision-making process. After you have gathered all the information you can, this type of provost wants you to give it to him or her, and then the provost will make the final decision. In this type of associate-provost–provost relationship, you serve merely as a messenger. The information you gather must be as accurate and complete as when you are making the decision.

DECISIONS INVOLVING STUDENTS

Most of the decisions you will face as an associate provost will center around a student's academic history or academic standing or both. When a department or college has a situation that cannot be resolved at its level, sometimes the situation will come to your desk.

Remember the section called "Decision Making 101," and consider the following basics about making decisions involving students:

- If a decision is needed about a grading situation, meet with the professors and instructors who are involved and gather needed information. Meet with the dean of the college or the director of the department to inform him or her that you will be involved in making a decision. Read the university's policy on grading and base your decision on policy. Inform the provost.
- If a decision is needed about whether a student remains at the university, reviewing the student's transcript is the first step. Look for the student's current grade point average, the number of times the student has taken a course, the number of semester credit hours the student has completed, the student's intended graduation year, and the student's degree plan. Arrange a meeting with the student when you have the needed information. After meeting with the student, as always, stay in contact with the academics in the department or college.
- Many of the decisions regarding students also involve their parents. First and foremost, check to see if the student has a form (Family Educational Rights and Privacy Act [FERPA]) in place that gives you permission to talk to the parents about their student. The university treats students as adults and as adults, parents aren't contacted. If a parent calls and wants to know what's taking place with his or her student, use kind words but let them know that you won't be able to tell them anything.

Each of the situations above may get a little touchy. Why? Students who have problems, such as the ones mentioned, tend to cry and be very concerned about what their fate might be. When you meet with such a student and have to decide whether the student can remain at the university, he or she tends to get emotional. Students tend to beg and plead with you not to tell their parents.

When you follow policy, when you gather information that reveals the student's actions do not put the student in a favorable light, or when a discipline issue requires immediate action, the decision you make has to be in the best interests of the academic community.

In some cases, with a student crying and begging, you might have a tendency to give the student another chance. The caring part of you will lean towards the decision to let the student stay in school even if the student's transcript shows he or she might need a break from university life or the student's grade point average is below the required 2.0 (check the university's policy about required grade point averages). Your heart cannot make the decision.

The associate provost part of you will look at the same data, ask the same questions, meet with the same student, and follow university policies. While you will certainly care about the student's well-being and will hope that the parents will be accepting of the student's situation, policy rules.

Your heart will be tugged when the student and the parent both want to meet with you. This tag-team approach is done in hopes of a favorable decision for the student.

Parents often present themselves as advocates for their child, regardless of what their student has done. Parents forget the real reason a decision is having to be made.

Parents forget the fact that their child failed to go to class and that resulted in a failing grade in that class. Parents don't want to hear that drugs were found in their child's dorm room. Parents want to believe what their child has told them. Parents want to believe that the professor was being unfair when he didn't accept the student's late work.

What parents don't want to see or hear about is what your collected information will reveal. Parents don't want to see an attendance record for their child that shows a lack of attendance in a class. Parents want to believe their child would never do drugs and never want to know their child has been untruthful.

During these very tense conversations, parents also want to know what is possible. If their student is removed from the university, when can the student return? Can the student enroll in another institution if the student is removed from yours? Can the student retake the class he or she failed? What is the cost of a repeated class? Be prepared with the answers and more.

Here's the thing to remember. The decision you make will impact the lives of the student and his or her family. It will impact financial considerations for the student and his or her family. When parents and students sit in your office and all they want is to find a way for their student to stay in school, you will tend to have sympathy for the situation, but keep in mind policies and consistency, for what you do for one student, you must do for all.

In some cases where a student is concerned, the professors in the student's area of study might actually seek you out to help them make a decision regarding the student staying in their program. Each program at the university has departmental guidelines. Certain classes have to be passed, and students have to maintain a set grade point average (usually 2.0).

When a student fails to meet the required 2.0 grade point average, the student is usually placed on probation and given another semester to improve his or her standing. If the same student fails to raise his or her grade point average during the probation period, the department can extend the student's probationary period or suspend the student. Every university has procedures and protocols for these situations.

Point to Ponder: If this type of situation comes to your desk, make sure the department's practices and protocols are aligned with university policy. Most decisions you have to make need to be made with university policies not departmental practices.

The department in question might seek your assistance because there is difference of opinion among faculty. Some faculty want to extend the probationary period and others want the student to be expelled. The dean has also asked for your input. When this occurs, go back to the process steps you developed in order to make difficult decisions.

This is one of those times when your recommendation will support the decision of the college, will follow policy, and will not have to reach the provost's level. Also, this is one of those times when, having reached a solution, you exhibit your decision-making skills to the provost. As mentioned before—and don't forget it—someone is always watching. Don't be anxious or worried. This kind of "watching" is done by others who need you to be good at problem solving, people like the provost and other administrators.

If a decision is needed about a discipline issue concerning a student and you are called in to represent the university, follow the same basic steps called for in the section called "Decision-Making 101": gather data, meet with the students and all other involved parties, collect more data, and follow policies.

How might a particular student discipline situation end up on your desk? Every college and university has a discipline committee that conducts hearings on student discipline issues. These issues could involve drug usage, threats, plagiarism, and any other situation that violates the university's code of student conduct. You may even be asked to serve as a member of this committee to, once again, represent campus administration.

For instance, a professor has verified that a student in her class has cheated on a test. After confronting the student with the evidence, the professor, the dean, and the department collectively recommended expulsion from the university. The case then was turned over to the university's discipline committee.

When a student is removed from a university because of a discipline issue, the student can leave with or without his or her transcript. Usually, leaving with a transcript means that the student can enroll in another university or college at the same academic point at which the student left your university (this depends on university policy). If a student is not allowed to have a transcript when the student is expelled, the student has to start over academically.

As the associate provost, you may be called in to make a final decision for the university in such a case. Once the data have been given to you and you have reviewed the data, you really need to ask a few questions:

1. Did the student violate the student code of conduct?;
2. Is suspension from the university a consequence for the violation?; and
3. Does the consequence meet the academic standards of the university?

There will be more questions to ask as you move through the disciplinary process. You'll learn more as you go. University decisions that involve students are not always easy to make. You and the university are in the business of educating students. Parents depend on the university to help their students complete a four-year degree and graduate as persons ready to enter their chosen workforce. Removing a student from the university brings a close to one part of a parent's dream for their child.

When those difficult decisions come your way, when a student cries and begs, and when you have to make a decision that does not support a faculty action, keep one thought in mind: All of your decisions are based on university policies. They are not made arbitrarily or capriciously, which means your decisions were not made from a "gut" feeling or on a whim.

DECISIONS INVOLVING PARENTS

Contacts and questions from parents can range from "My son has how many parking tickets?" to "Why isn't my daughter graduating?" Even though parents were told at the very first parents' meeting that the university would treat their student as an adult and any concern that arose would be addressed between the student and the institution, memories fail when baby boy calls mama.

The very first thing to remember when dealing with a parent is that there is a story the parent heard from his or her child about what took place and then there is the university's side of the story. The story from the university's side hopefully comes from collected data. If you are very lucky, these stories will match and the parent is only trying to find possible solutions.

You also need to be prepared for parents that doesn't want to listen to your "excuses" about why their baby is having so many problems at your institution. According to such parents, whatever has happened is the fault of the university. What steps might you take if and when this happens? Remember, in such situations, parents sometimes call the president.

- When parents are ranting at you, be sure to get their name and the name of their student. You can always find contact information through university records.
- Don't tell such parents that you understand their situation. You don't.
- Let such parents finish telling their story. When they have finished, let them know you are in a position to help find a solution.
- Inform such parents that you are unfamiliar with the situation and it will take some time to gather all the information possible.
- Begin collecting information about the situation.
- Give the parents your office number in case they need to call you.
- Ask for at least forty-eight hours to gather some data.
- Call the parents back with what you have found.
- Work with the parents to find a solution.

The hopeful outcome is that you will be able to help parents, establish a positive relationship with them, and also assist a student with a concern.

How about another practice exercise regarding decisions with parents?

Parent call to ask why their student is failing a particular class. The provost asks you to look into the matter. You search the student's records and find out that there is no FERPA form on file. There is nothing you can legally tell the parents. You contact the parents and tell them that, without a FERPA form, you cannot give out any academic information.

Because college students are usually eighteen years of age or older, they are considered adults. This means they have the rights and responsibilities of adults. Parents can request and obtain any academic information about their adult student as long as the student has completed a FERPA form. Without this form in place, parents cannot obtain academic information about their students from the university. This often times makes parents very angry, unhappy, and disgruntled.) In your scenario, the parents, who are clearly upset with this decision, threaten to meet with the president, to talk with a board-of-regents member, and to call a newspaper with the story of how they have been mistreated. All of this could happen except for the fact that you and the institution have set certain standards in place. So, consider the following facts:

- The president is a very busy person; that is why the president hands these issues to the provost who, in turn, hands them to you. It is very unlikely a parent will be able to see the president about a grade issue.
- In essence, a board-of-regents member's authority exists only when the board is convened. Calling such a board member usually results in the president getting another call, and we know what happens after that.

- If a newspaper is contacted, the university usually has a media communications department that will address the situation. If this is the case, let that particular department handle the concern and issue an institutional reply.

Before responding to parents and after you have checked to see that a FERPA form is in place, return to your decision-making process. Parents' reactions to certain situations differ drastically from those of their children. Some believe that, since they are paying tuition for their child to attend your university, they are a little special.

So, here are a few guidelines that might come in handy in situations like the above scenario:

- If parents ask to talk with the professor, give them the professor's email address, not the professor's office phone number. Be sure to call or email the professor with a heads up that a parent might be calling.
- If parents asks you if your decision is the final one, be sure to let them know you have a position in which you can help them. If they don't like that response, you can always direct them to the provost. Regardless, be sure to tell them policies will be followed and let the provost know what might be coming his or her way.
- If parents starts to bargain with you by saying that they will make a large contribution to the university or that they will tell all of their friends that your university is the place to be, disregard this conversation. You will help with their child's situation because it's the right thing to do.

Building positive relationships with parents is of great importance to the university system. Parents can be spokespersons for the academics that take place at the university. They can bring prospective students and potential donors to the institution. They are invaluable. With that said, not every request they make can be granted. Always be kind, helpful, and respectful, and handle as much as you can before a situation escalates.

DECISIONS INVOLVING FACULTY

This particular category of decision making is a little touchy because you have to work side-by-side with faculty members everyday while serving as the associate provost. As a newly employed associate provost, your reputation as a policy follower and faculty advocate are in the developmental phase. Keep this thought in the back of your mind when you are assigned the task of investigating any situation having to do with faculty.

The areas for decision-making when dealing with faculty usually stem from student situations, curriculum and program needs, situations that arise between faculty members, and possibly university decisions.

If you don't know already, faculty are very protective of their colleagues and their programs. So, when student situations come to the surface, faculty have their departmental rules and university policies to fall back on. Professors may select their teaching style, means of communicating with students, and grading practices as long as these attributes can be supported by policies.

Ready for another practice scenario addressing decisions with faculty?

A situation involving faculty advising comes to the attention of the provost. Apparently, faculty advisors are not up to date on current curriculum changes and have been advising students to take courses that are no longer in their degree plans. The provost asks you to gather some information and see what's taking place and if there is a viable solution.

The first thing to do is to bring the situation to the deans of the colleges. The deans may or may not be aware of the advising situation that is taking place. Also, some faculty are assigned advising duties and may not have regular advising roles in their colleges. However, because of these misadvising sessions, some students are taking unnecessary and oftentimes duplicate courses.

Some of the faculty advisors are very upset that they have been singled out as being a primary cause of students taking unnecessary courses. They have gone to their deans, complaining that they were unaware of the relevant curriculum changes and that they don't like having an associate provost interfering in their departments.

Since the provost has given you the task of finding a solution, you automatically move into your problem-solving process. You do the following:

- Gather information. Get your ducks in a row because a goal of yours is to develop positive relationships with faculty.
- After informing the deans that you have been asked to inquire about this situation, arrange a meeting with the named faculty advisors to get their side of the story. Collect the data.
- Arrange a meeting with advisors from various academic departments across the university to determine the process for curriculum changes in their colleges. Collect the data.
- Arrange a meeting with the university curriculum committee to determine when curriculum changes take place and how those changes are communicated to the colleges. Collect the data.
- After you gather the information, prepare an information sheet for the provost with possible suggestions and recommendations to address the concern.

- Some possible recommendations for the provost might include
- forming a university-wide committee of advisors,
- identifying a person on the university's curriculum committee to be responsible for informing the colleges, especially faculty advisors, when curriculum changes take place,
- asking the professional advisors to hold an informational meeting with faculty advisors, and
- asking deans to appoint willing faculty members to be advisors.
- But, first, don't forget the cardinal act when dealing with a program or faculty member. Regardless of the situation, you always contact the dean of that college and inform the dean that you are dealing with a situation that involves one of their faculty. This can be easily done with a simple email or phone call. The deans will appreciate your informing them about situations that are taking place in their colleges.

BITING YOUR TONGUE; MAKING TOUGH BUT RIGHT DECISION

Your position as an associate provost provides you with the ability to attend various very important meetings. In some of these meetings, decisions that you don't agree with might be made. Sometimes, with the knowledge you have, you may know a decision isa wrong move for a department, a college, or even the university to take.

With what you know, you really want to raise your hand and state your opinion, an opinion that might not be in your purview to express. If you have been very smart in your work with the provost, you have already informed the provost of your opinion and it might differ from the decision that is going to be made.

Here comes the hard part. You can disagree behind a closed door about a situation or a decision being made in the provost's office. But you never—pay very close attention to these words—you never openly disagree with the provost in a meeting or in front of other administrators. It is in your best interests to keep personal opinions to yourself until you can have a one-on-one meeting with the provost.

Depending on your desire to have a long run as an associate provost, there comes a time when it's best to bite your tongue and keep opinions to yourself. Discernment is essential when making the decision to hold your tongue and wait to express your disapproval of a decision or an opinion. This doesn't mean you can't have an opinion or your own thoughts; just pick the best time for sharing.

So, when might discernment come into play? Here are a few situations when it would be in your best interest to keep your opinions to yourself:

- If you are in a meeting with the provost and others and one of the people in the meeting decides to say something you disagree with, write yourself a note to bring the point up at a different time, possibly in a one-on-one meeting with that particular person. Be sure to let the provost know about that conversation.
  - **Note to Self:** Don't have open arguments in front of others, no matter what the disagreement is about. It's OK to disagree in a friendly manner but not to argue.
- If you are at a professional meeting with administrators (other provosts, university presidents and vice presidents, or deans) and a situation arises that causes you to take offense or that makes you want to openly disagree with what was said, make sure your comments are appropriate and well timed.
  - **Note to Self**: No one said you have to be made of stone and let people make fun of your institution or its people. Just find the right time and, possibly with a little humor, give back a little of what you received. Sarcasm is often very helpful.
- If the provost asks you to give your opinion about something, especially in a general meeting, remember to be truthful but gracious. The provost might really be asking you to support one of his or her own decisions.
  - **Note to Self:** Try to state your opinions in the form of suggestions or recommendations instead of an out-and-out disagreement. This type of response shows support for the provost and, at the same time, gives you a chance to state some personal opinions.

You know yourself and how you respond to certain situations better than anyone else knows. If you fly off the handle easily or take certain comments personally, find a way to curtail the impulse to speak out of turn. Wait for a time to talk privately to the provost. You can have opinions and they can differ from others' opinions. Proper timing and good word choices are essential to maintaining your position as a dependable associate provost.

LET'S LOOK BACK

With a myriad of situations coming at you from every corner of the university, you need to develop a process for addressing decisions that need to be made. You need to commit to follow that plan every time the need to make a decision comes to your desk, whether from a student, a parent, a faculty member, or the provost—especially the provost.

By now, you already know that correct data collection is imperative, staying in communication with all parties is not a choice but a requirement, and the provost has to be involved either first-hand or through written communications. You also know not to make decisions based on your feelings, such as feeling sorry for a student who has gotten himself into a bad situation. University decisions, at your level, are made by following policies, striving for a workable solution, and embracing the best interests of the institution.

Just for questioning's sake, what food did you decide to try when you were at the fair? The "Motherclucker" chicken sandwich did sound pretty tasty. And how could you have missed the fried Twinkie booth? Decisions at the fair about the food you want to try are not complicated. With a system in place to help you make decisions as an associate provost and with university policies in mind, those decisions will become easier to make.

LET'S TALK ABOUT THE REAL WORLD

Having opinions is not always a bad thing. Sharing opinions doesn't mean you are in the wrong. And, in some cases, the provost might actually rely on you to voice some opinions. Also, don't forget that making decisions, while not printed on a job requirement list, is an essential part of your responsibilities as the associate provost.

When making decisions on behalf of the provost and making decisions affecting the university, always keep in the back of your mind some primary questions:

- How will my decision impact others and the university?
- Will my decision change some workings of the institution? If so, how?
- Are the decisions I make being made based on university policies?
- Do I have the support of the provost?

These are all valid questions. Further, here is some real-world language: Don't be a wuss! Yes, you read that right. Fear or worry can't prevent you from making difficult decisions. Being wishy-washy serves no purpose and can waste valuable time. Just make those decisions in the best way possible: thinking of others and the institution. If you have to use a hammer to solve a situation, use one made of velvet.

WHAT WOULD YOU DO?

Making decisions that affect all aspects of the university will sometimes fall to you, especially if the provost assigns you a situation that needs attention. The scenario below presents you with a situation that needs a resolution. Possible action steps are provided for you to choose from and are not listed in any specific order.

The curriculum-selection process is taking place on the campus. This means that faculty and departments have the opportunity to submit new programs and courses and make requests to delete or modify courses or programs. The provost has asked you to sit on the university's curriculum committee.

At one of the meetings of the university curriculum committee, a college announces that it has decided to delete a course. This course has been used by another college to meet a requirement of one of its degrees. The college that is deleting the course is also requesting a new course be added. However, the new course that is being added does not fit into the other college's degree plan. These changes thus present a problem for the other college.

To address this situation and find a solution, consider some of the actions listed below:

- __ Ask for the degree plans for each of the programs.
- __ Determine if the course being deleted is part of the forty-two-hour core course requirements.
- __ Review the information about the new course.
- __ Discuss the intent for removing the course from the program offering.
- __ Discuss the intent for adding the new course instead of keeping the previous course.
- __ Determine if the program that still needs the course can find a substitute course in another program.
- __ Ask each of the colleges to develop new degree plans showing how the newly recommended course impacts each program.
- __ Keep the provost informed.
- __ Be cognizant of timelines associated with curriculum issues.

Chapter 7

Visiting the Petting Zoo (Building Positive Relationships with Internal and External Entities)

One of the most visited exhibits at the State Fair of Texas is the petting zoo. There are baby animals everywhere, and all of them are hungry. These animals move around their pens just waiting for someone to put out their hands with some little green alfalfa pellets.

This particular part of the fairgrounds is always filled with children and their families as they move around various pens and pet the baby animals. The smell is not always fragrant. and some of the baby goats like to take a little nip out of tiny hands now and then. Regardless of the smell and the little nips here and there, the petting zoo is always crowded. The animals appear to be healthy and well cared for. The petting zoo, really, not a bad setup: various types of animals, living in the same pens, and in a friendly place.

When you enter the petting zoo, you notice a definite path, a sort of natural flow. You move towards the baby llamas in a stream-like procession with others in the crowd. What you also notice is that very few people, if any, diverge from the established path. The crowd of strangers simply knows what to do to get along and enjoy the exhibit. Such is the way of building internal and external relationships as an associate provost.

How does the visit to the petting zoo correlate to your work as a newly appointed associate provost who has been charged with building positive relationships with internal and external entities? The petting zoo relies on friendly people coming in, moving along a well-organized path, and treating all of the animals with kindness and gentleness. Such is your charge when working with internal and external entities: Look for friendly people, help them gain an understanding of how university systems work, and treat all people with kindness.

THE INSTITUTION AS A BUSINESS

You should realize that one of the most important aspects of a university, beyond it being an institution of higher education, is it being a business. Additionally, you should know that, internal and external entities help this business function and that your building positive relationships with these entities is essential. Remember, in every situation in your role, you represent the university. Basically, you are as much of a business partner with the university as the external and internal entities are.

Understanding the university as a business doesn't happen overnight. Your schedule is packed with meetings, completing tasks assigned by the provost, and working with the departments under your purview. Remember that you as an associate provost are at the center of helping the institution prosper, the students succeed, and the reputation of the academic community increase.

With the mindset that the university is a business and you are part of the business, here are some basic facts that you might want to remember:

- The academic side of the house needs to work hand-in-hand with the university side of the house. Many academic and university programs are connected by the services provided to students. Working together saves time and energy for both sides of the house.
- Some internal entities do not have established working budgets and must rely on their requested job assignments to fund many of their operations. This simple business model is often not understood by faculty and staff members and is why, before a job assignment can be completed, such an internal entity has to have a budget code from a department that does have an established budget.
- The department of athletics, most of the time, has a bigger and better budget than any academic department. While this fact is usually broadly known, many faculty members have a hard time accepting the comparatively limited budgets of their departments. However, athletics is still considered an internal entity, one that brings in a lot of revenue to the university.
- The students and their families are the customers and should be helped as much as possible. Increasing student enrollment is essential to keeping the university in the business of higher education. The goal of every recruitment effort is to increase student enrollment, in essence, to "grow the business."
- Employees matter, no matter where they serve or the rank they hold. You will not be able to change their pay scales or offer more days off, but you

can work with staff members to create a positive working environment that shows your appreciation for all they do.

- The university's operational budgets can never go in the red. This is not wishful thinking; rather, this is a state mandate. The yearly budget must be balanced before the end of the fiscal year. The university never wants to be in a position in which monies have to be paid back. Being in such a situation would affect many academic departments and university offices across the campus.
- Evaluation assessments of academic programs, university departments, and every person who works at the university occur constantly. You will be required to complete evaluations for staff members in the departments assigned to you every year, and you will be involved with many program evaluations. Just as in any business, reviews are completed to ensure a company and its people are goal oriented and focused on improvements.

The entities mentioned above exemplify only a few of the ways in which your institution works within a business model. Monies are made available but have to be accounted for. Some departments mentioned above depend on others for their continued work efforts. Further, whether they work at McDonald's, in the athletic department, or in an academic office, people matter.

Larry Page, the cofounder of Google, said, "Always deliver more than expected." He was so right. In the business world, especially at a university, the delivery of more than what is expected could make a difference when students and their families are making decisions about where to go to earn their four-year degrees or when future employees make decisions about where they want to work.

IDENTIFYING AND WORKING
WITH INTERNAL ENTITIES

In previous chapters, internal entities have been mentioned in conjunction with some of the duties you face in your role as an associate provost. Some of the internal entities with which you will be working on a regular basis include:

- the business office,
- the financial-aid office,
- the parking and traffic department,
- the maintenance and grounds department,
- the registrar's office,
- the human resources department,

- the residential life office,
- the library services department,
- the information technology services department,
- the student center personnel (food services),
- the bookstore, and
- the admissions office.

These are just a few of the internal entities with which you will work. At this point, you might be wiping your brow, bowing your head in a silent prayer, and talking to yourself. To make you feel a little better, you won't have to work with all of the above every day. However, the work that you do with these entities is vital. More importantly, the positive relationships you build with the people in these areas are essential to your success as an associate provost.

For you to have a base of knowledge about these offices and departments from a collective frame of mind, you need to be aware of the following commonalities that run through each of them:

- Many of these offices employ staff members, and staff members are considered at-will employees. At-will employees can be dismissed from university services for any reason.
- Most staff members are paid by the hour. This is why you will see most of them still working in their offices during holiday breaks. Some staff members have to take vacation days to be off during holiday closures.
- Most of these staff members, when first hired, work for at least ninety days on a probationary basis.
- Some of the staff members who work in the academic areas may know who you are and the position you hold. A goal of yours should be being known for the work you are doing and not for your position as one of the university administrators.
- Many of the staff members in these offices and departments are specialists in their respective areas. You should be cognizant of their ability to be helpful in assisting you.
- Most importantly, know that, to be successful in your role, especially when providing services to parents and students, you need these staff members more than they need you.

Your university has all of these offices and more. Many people, with the exact number depending on the size of your institution, work in each of these areas. As much as it will benefit you to know as many staff members as possible, time constraints may not allow you to know all of them. In that case, as early as you can, identify at least one contact person from each of these internal entities to be your "go-to" person.

INTERNAL ENTITIES BEHIND THE SCENES

Think back to a previous chapter when two sides of the house were mentioned. The house in this instance refers to the university as a whole. You, as the associate provost, work on the academic side of the house. The university side of the house refers to other university offices that are not academic in nature. These offices and their people are also considered internal entities.

While your day is filled with certain academic duties and responsibilities, the staff members in these nonacademic internal offices work endlessly to keep the business of the university running as smoothly as possible. Below are just a few nonacademic internal entities you should know and know well.

The **admissions office** is one of those internal entities that you will probably come to know very well and is one of the most important and essential offices at the university. As with any of the offices on the campus that you will be working with, you need to establish a contact person from that office.

As an associate provost, one of your goals is increasing student enrollment. Therefore, you will probably be directly involved with enrollment efforts and may oftentimes speak for the university as part of enrollment efforts. You might also have knowledge of various academic programs across the colleges, and such knowledge is useful in enrollment-boosting activities.

If your provost has delegated, as one of your regular duties, assistance in the area of enrollment efforts, you may find yourself attending recruitment events at various high schools and community colleges, arranging meetings with various academics from other institutions, or spending some afternoons welcoming potential students to the university.

During these times, many questions arise concerning entrance qualifications, acceptance of transfer credits, and general academic questions. This is why you, as an administrator with knowledge of faculty and programs, will be helpful. Basically, you can run interference for potential students, connect them to academic departments, and direct them to the appropriate university offices.

An important university responsibility that is often held by the admissions office is connecting high-school students with dual credit offerings at the university. If you are not familiar with dual credit, it involves connecting high-school curriculum with university courses, enabling students to graduate from high school with earned college credit.

Many times, high-school students can take at least sixty hours of college credit. Any time you can be a part of an enrollment effort, such participation sends a subliminal message to others that the administrative side of the house is present and committed to enrollment efforts. Your role may be one of providing help to students by putting them in touch with expert academic advisors who will assist with degree planning.

Another office that sometimes gets forgotten but can be one of the most helpful to students is the **financial-aid office**. This office can help you help a student stay in school by providing them with additional funding. This office can literally save a student's academic future after receiving just one phone call from an associate provost.

Students who find their way to your office because of financial need usually have lost their financial aid because of failing grades. Others have let the deadline for paying their tuition pass or have experienced some previous financial woes. In your position, you will be able to call your contact person in the financial-aid office and get an itemized report on the student's financial-aid history. The report details when the student received financial aid, when the bill was paid, and how much the student currently owes the university.

When a student comes to your office and presents a financial-aid problem, there are a few steps that you can take to help the student address his or her financial-aid situation:

- Call the financial-aid office and ask for a report on the student's financial-aid history.
- Ask someone, hopefully the director of the department, to create a summary report of the history statement.
- Ask the director to detail possible options for the student. Options depend on the student's grade point average and financial status at this time.
- Contact the student and inform the student of the details of his or her current status.
- Direct the student to the financial-aid office for further assistance, if needed.

Another important part of working with the financial-aid office is knowing that sometimes, even in your position as an associate provost, you cannot help a student. Some offices, such as the financial-aid office, have certain state and federal guidelines that they must adhere to. If the financial-aid office does not adhere to such guidelines, state and federal entities may significantly reduce the monies they provide to the university. So, if you are told there is nothing that can be done, respect the response and share the information with the student, using that velvet hammer you have to use sometimes.

If you are not familiar with the workings of the **registrar's office**, you will be. Usually this office works with graduation procedures, confirms the completion of degrees, and issues diplomas. When a student, a parent, a faculty member, or the provost has a concern in one of these areas, the registrar's office is the place to find the answers. If you have not had much involvement with this particular office, you need to learn as much about it as you can.

When it comes to completing a degree, students become very anxious. Why is the tube you get at graduation oftentimes empty? Because the registrar's office has to verify the completion of your degree requirements and that cannot be done until final grades have been posted and that usually happens after graduation. Who else makes anxious phone calls? That's right, parents do. And to whom do anxious parents usually direct their calls? Again, you are right, they direct their calls to the president. You already know where that anxious parent's phone call will end up.

Those anxious students are seeking employment after graduation and need their diplomas. Until the degrees are finally conferred, students may call or come by your office in a state of panic. All that's needed is a quick call to the registrar's office to confirm that the student has completed all the requirements for the degree. Once this has been confirmed, the registrar can issue a letter from the university, indicating the status of the student. This action will suffice until the diploma is sent to the student. Also, a transcript showing when the degree was conferred can be provided.

Another responsibility that often falls to the registrar's office is the review of degree plans. Because of your work with academics, this essential process is relevant to your work. This office reviews degree plans from other institutions to ensure students have an easy transition into your university when transferring credits from another institution. This office usually reads course descriptions from each institution to confirm approval of substitutions.

The offices mentioned above are all found on the other side, the nonacademic side, of the house, and the staff that work in these offices and others are vital to the workings of the university. An earlier chapter recommended showing kindness and respect for those who work at the university. Doing so will help you establish a firm foundation of friendship with campus personnel. And the friendships you develop will, in turn, help students stay in school.

For dealing with other offices that help you help students, such as the offices of admissions and financial aid, you need to regularly use the following specific qualities, some of which you probably already possess:

- Confirming stories: Most of the people in these offices have heard a variety of students' stories. So, if a student comes to your office with an "odd-but-true" story about a conversation that took place in one of the campus offices, be sure to call that office and get the real story.

Hopefully, the student has been honest with you, and that department can be of assistance.

- Requests: When a staff member from one of these offices comes to you with a request or favor, do what you can to help. At your level, you can pull a few strings. You will begin to grow a feeling of trust with the office, trust that will help to solidify emerging relationships.
- Kindness: Always be kind—enough said.

The above recommendations are simple, yet they are always factors in building positive relationships with other internal entities on the campus. Whether you are working with the food services department or the parking and traffic department, these suggestions still apply. Verifying stories, asking for supporting data about certain situations, and having both sides of the house working in tandem all translates to helping students in the best ways possible.

SHARING A FEW WORDS

Some situations will leave you at a loss for words. What do you say to an angry parent? How do you use your words to comfort a student who has received some heartbreaking news about his academic status? How do you say supportive words to a faculty member who has created a difficult situation for you? Your replies need to be succinct and clear. You always want to avoid miscommunications from taking place with internal and external entities.

For your role as an associate provost, there isn't a script or even a set of Cliff Notes to follow. Every word you say needs to be as correct as possible. If you make a parent angrier, will he or she call the president? You betcha. If you disagree with a dean on a particular matter, will the provost find out? Most definitely.

As you learn your way around your role and your interactions with internal and external entities, it might be nice for you to have at least some responsive statements at your disposal. Knowing that your words have lives of their own, here are a few statements for you to choose from, statements that might help you in various situations. You may need to use only a few of these until your own words set the tone for responding to those in the academic community.

- Delivering messages from the provost:
- "The provost wants you to know he is aware of your current situation and will address it as soon as he can."
- "The provost is working on a possible solution for the situation you just brought to his attention."

- "The provost wants you to know that a decision is being made and as soon as he can meet with you, he will."
- Department requests:
- "The provost wants you to know that she is aware of your request and she is looking for a viable resource to help you."
- "If the provost can help in any way, I feel certain she will."
- "I know you are looking for an answer and, when the provost makes a decision, either she or I will contact you."
- "I know you are expecting an answer from the provost. The provost needs a few days to provide you with a solution to your request."
- Request or questions from a faculty member:
- "I know you have been waiting for a response from the provost. When I meet with the provost, I will make sure this issue gets to him again."
- "The provost and the other administrators have been very involved in getting the board meeting packets together. As soon as I have a chance, I will ask the provost about the state of your concern."
- "As soon as the provost gives me the go-ahead with a response, I will be happy to get back with you."

Of course, these are not the only responses to choose from. Of course, your communications with internal entities in the academic community need to foster growing positive working relationships. Hopefully, you and the provost have already discussed certain procedures to take when faced with some of the above situations. If so, follow the provost's lead and be sure to avoid trite or insincere responses.

BRINGING IN THE OUTSIDE: WORKING WITH SURROUNDING EXTERNAL ENTITIES

External entities include any group or organization that works in conjunction with the efforts of the organization. Basically, these entities live outside the realm of the university but definitely have a direct influence on its workings. Whether you are directed to do so by the provost or not, make it a point to reach out to these external entities as early as possible.

When you start this effort, begin with the community surrounding the university. As a member of the administration at the university, you will often be called upon to attend community functions, which may include holiday festivals, Rotary Club meetings, and volunteer community-service projects.

In some cases, the provost may actually ask you to attend some of these events to represent the university, so making contact with external entities early in your tenure will be beneficial. Consider this request as a means of connecting your institution to the community. Your presence sends a message that the university cares about what is happening in the community.

When attending these events, be aware of the following ways that you can acclimate yourself to being a member of both the university and the community:

- Introduce yourself with your first name and the institution where you serve. Don't say where you "work" because it's more than work; it's service. Then ask others their names, where they are from, and what they do. Take a moment to share positive stories about the university and offer them an open invitation to visit the university.
- Carry your business cards with you to every event. On the back of each card, write a specific note that mentions the name of the event and how nice it was to meet them. A card might read, "I enjoyed seeing you at this year's Downtown Merchant's Fair," followed by your name. Your business card tells your position, and a personal note brings a human side to meeting community members.
- Wear school colors and clothing with the university's name on it to every event.
- If a community leadership program is offered, join it. This course will not only strengthen your leadership skills but also provide opportunities to meet people from all walks of the community. Networking opportunities such as this often bring positive rewards to the university.
- Offer the use of university space (with permission, of course) for community events (University Interscholastic League competitions, cheerleader camps). There are open spaces all over the campus and in several buildings. Bringing community members to the campus gives them an inside look at one of the largest employers in the community.
- When creating university committees that require a community presence, reach out to those you met at community events and invite them to be members of such committees.
- If you don't live in the community where the university is located, be sure to read the area newspaper. You may read it online, using the university's subscription, or at the local library, which usually carries local newspapers. Such reading keeps you updated on the people living and the things happening in the community.

In addition to being a part of community events, when you take on the position of associate provost, be sure to introduce yourself to area realtors, local school-district officials, and local medical personnel. If your institution is in a metropolitan area, making such introductions might be a little difficult, so start small with the community members closest to the university. When you are more acquainted with the area, attend more events and meet more people.

As you become more familiar with your role at the university and continue your efforts to ingrain yourself with what's taking place in the community, you don't have to accept every invitation that comes to you—unless, of course, it comes from the provost. Despite needing to attend many events and meet many people, you might actually decline attending an event where kissing pigs is in order.

PLAYING NICE WITH OTHER INSTITUTIONS OF HIGHER EDUCATION

You will work not only with other community entities but also with other institutions of higher education, such as community colleges and other four-year universities. Remember how this chapter started by detailing how an educational institution is a business? As in any industry, there is a sense of friendly competition in higher education.

The competition centers around institutions' efforts to increase their own student enrollment. Personnel members in university admissions offices exert a great deal of energy visiting high schools and community colleges, selling the wonderful points about their institution and its high academic standing. When your institution's staff members are visiting all of these places, so are the staff members of other colleges and universities.

In working with external entities, one of the most important connections you can make is with community colleges. Many community colleges have two-year degree programs and produce graduates who have completed associate degrees and are seeking to enroll in a university that has four-year degree programs.

The primary goal is to help create academic pathways for community-college graduates. Why not let your university be the place for such graduates to continue their studies?

If you are lucky, the provost will assign you the duty of working with admissions-office staff members as they outreach to high schools and community colleges. This work provides you with a wonderful opportunity to work hand-in-hand with high-school counselors, to use the university's academic advisors to assist in degree planning to prevent students from taking any unnecessary courses, and to showcase the many academic programs your university offers.

As an academic, there are a few reasons why you might want to take an active role in working with the admissions office. Your work with this endeavor

- allows you to stay in contact with academic advisors,
- assist students with career choices,
- help students make academic connections at the university, and
- provides you with an opportunity to work in tandem with external entities from high schools and community colleges.

Another opportunity that may present itself when working with external entities is that of connecting your academic institution with another institution. If the provost assigns this task to you, first be aware that this task is assigned in addition to those already on your list. However, this duty is essential to your becoming an integral part of the academic community. As a newly appointed associate provost, you may or may not have had experiences in planning this kind of academic meeting.

Here are a few possible steps for your consideration:

- The easiest way to connect with community colleges is very simple (if your institution does not already have a relationship with a two-year institution). Call your counterpart at the community college and let her know your institution would be interested in partnering with her institution, especially with specific programs.For instance, your university may have a very successful education program. Graduates from the community college may want to pursue their teaching degree. Your institution's program might be just the one to help these students become future teachers.
- Once initial contacts have been made, invite representatives from the community college to visit your campus to speak with academics from a variety of colleges and programs.
- In your initial conversations with community college folks, determine the academic focus for the meeting. For instance, if the community college has graduates that are interested in the sciences, invite the dean and department chairpersons from the college of mathematics and sciences. Be sure to ask the chairpersons to provide copies of several degree plans.
- Before representatives of both institutions agree on a time, day, and place for this meeting, be sure to check with the provost and the president. While their attendance at the meeting might be brief, make sure their attendance is possible.
- When planning for the meeting, just as with any meeting, contact the parking department to ensure open parking spaces for the visitors, arrange for a meeting place, contact food services to arrange for refreshments, including, possibly, a lunch depending on the meeting time, and contact the admissions office for "goodies" to hand out when the visitors depart.

- Once representatives of both institutions decide on the day, place, and time, be sure to send an official invitation to the community-college invitees at least two weeks before the actual meeting. Be sure to ask about the number of attendees that will be coming to the meeting on your campus. The same invitation should also go to the invitees from your university.
  - Create an agenda that has the time allotments, places, and names of those involved. The below items could be points on an agenda:General greeting by the provost or the president or both
  - Introduction of campus visitors and the academic teams
  - Meeting with all academics in a general setting
  - Breakout sessions for academic groups
  - Lunch or other refreshments (depending on the time of the meeting)
  - Final meeting to regroup for takeaways" from the meeting (use chart paper to collect notes)
  - Closing remarks
- After the meeting and in a timely manner, collect the notes from the debriefing session and send them to all of the attendees at the meeting.
- As always, provide a debriefing summary of the meeting to the provost. This can be done with a summary sheet or in person. The provost will want to share this with the president.

Your presence, as in other cases, at these functions is essential to show the commitment your institution has to the endeavor of connecting the academics and their programs to students in ways that will help students complete their degrees. These institutional meetings are usually very successful and open many doors for students from both universities.

Other four-year institutions are also entities with which to form positive relationships. You will meet several of your colleagues from these institutions at academic conferences and official meetings. At the very least, these meetings provide you with a networking system that is invaluable not only for you but also for your institution.

Even though the world of higher education is a competitive business, having connections with other four-year universities helps students who wish to transfer and assists in preplanning for degree audits and in advising incoming students. Playing nice with external entities is extremely important for the institution and for establishing yourself as an effective associate provost.

LET'S LOOK BACK

The internal and external entities mentioned in this chapter are only a few of the entities you will be working with in your role. When it comes to planning, you have to become an expert or be fortunate enough to have exceptional assistance.

Depending on the needs, academic or otherwise, that arise, the staff members of university offices are experts in their specific areas and stand ready to help. Every time these staff members provide assistance at your request may mean a student can stay in school or have more opportunities. It might be a zoo, but it's your zoo.

Petting zoos are always fun. The animals are always happy and eager to be fed, and most of the visitors are smiling and can't wait to pet a baby goat. At the same time, there are a few children shrieking because they aren't so happy to be there and have their picture taken with a camel who spit on them. It really comes down to the way the animals get treated.

Think about this analogy when you are building positive relationships with internal and external entities. Feed them, treat them with kindness, and make them feel special. Some of the people you deal with may act like animals every once in a while. Treating everyone from the president to a custodian with kindness goes a long way and so does offering little green alfalfa pellets.

LET'S TALK ABOUT THE REAL WORLD

When working with internal entities, every effort you make will help to build your credibility with the provost and the academic community. Your comebacks will be appropriate, well timed, and provost approved. Serving as an associate provost does give you some leeway when responding to others.

Anytime the provost wants to assign you new tasks, such as working with external entities, be aware that this and other additional duties take up time in your regularly scheduled day and week. Having processes in place and dedicated contacts in university offices will save you a great deal of time when addressing student, faculty, and university concerns.

In the real world, when you deal with internal and external entities, not everyone will follow the rules you have to follow because of your position. Just a reminder, when you feel the need to crawl across a table and tell someone what he can do with his nasty little comments, don't. When staff and faculty members feel they have no voice or are unappreciated, they tend to say and do things out of frustration. You might be in the line of fire. Take one for the team.

WHAT WOULD YOU DO?

Some of the internal and external entities you will work with in your role have been mentioned in this chapter. Of course, there are many more. The scenario below gives you a chance to work through planning an event for an internal entity. Several possible actions have been provided in no particular order. The intent is for you to work through a situation to find a possible solution.

The provost has asked you to serve on the New Faculty Orientation Committee. This internal committee is responsible for the orientation of new faculty members at the beginning of every fall term. The provost has given you some specific objectives, including making some changes within this committee and in some events organized by this committee, such as an evening reception held in honor of new faculty members. The reception also serves as a time when the president can meet with all new faculty members. The provost is expecting your service on the committee to bring about much-needed changes.

Using your honed skills as a master problem solver, review the following list of possible actions steps and bring a solution to the provost:

- __ Meet with the provost to clarify the provost's expectations.
- __ Arrange a meeting with the existing New Faculty Orientation Meeting members.
- __ Establish a date and create an agenda for the orientation meeting.
- __ Establish a place for the orientation and reception.
- __ Be sure all needed internal and external entities are represented on the committee.
- __ Check with the president's administrative assistant to determine an open evening for the president to attend the reception.
- __ Work with the committee to determine a schedule for all entities to have presentation times.
- __ Create an invitation for the event and send it to all new faculty members.
- __ Arrange for parking passes for all attendees.
- __ Arrange refreshments for both the meeting and the reception.
- __ Create an information pamphlet that details the contact information, departments, and ranking for all new faculty members for the president and the provost.

Chapter 8

Under the Big Top (Living in the World of University Administration)

One of the most visited places at the State Fair of Texas is the circus. Its main tent, the "big top," is just waiting for the next group of visitors to come and enjoy the animal acts, the clowns, and people swinging from the very top of the tent. It is a site of sequential and truly expertly timed events.

The three rings under the big top work simultaneously with each other. All the acts are taking place at the same time. The animals stay in their ring, prancing about; the clowns drive little cars, throw confetti paper into the crowd, and juggle little balls; and the aerial artists fly about as if they had wings. The timing of each act is precise. All participants know what to do and when to do it. They live and work under the big top and so will you.

The big top in an institution of higher education is its administration and its administrators. The administrative team usually includes the president, the vice presidents, the provost, associate provosts, and the legal team for the university. At your institution, there may be more players under the big top. You need to learn who these folks are, their positions, and their importance to the institution.

BIG PICTURE

Previous chapters have mentioned the various people and offices that keep the university in working order. Deans, department chairpersons, and faculty members are responsible for the university's academic work. The reason a provost is usually referred to as the vice president of academic affairs is because the provost serves as the appointed leader of academic endeavors.

You, as an associate provost, work at the direction of the provost. Your focus, like the provost's, is on academics. However, that does not mean that you won't be involved with student success, campus visits, state and national organizations, all kinds of meetings, and various operational efforts for the university. Basically, you could be all over the campus, involved with a variety of departments, and still working with and for other administrators.

To understand the big picture of a university, all the parts (departments, offices, functions) have to be looked at as a whole and from top to bottom. The previous chapters have introduced you to those who work at various levels of the university. Not all of them serve next to the president, the vice presidents, and the provost. You will.

While your efforts are focused on academics, the university is still working around you.

The groundskeepers are constantly refreshing campus flower beds and otherwise enhancing the campus's appearance. Maintenance workers are traveling across the campus, taking care of buildings and doing various projects. Admissions-office personnel are hosting visiting students and their families. Students are moving in between classes almost all day long. There is always something going on.

Understanding the university's big picture also means that you have to define the meaning of your role and the place you hold on the administrative team. This understanding and meaning do not come because of the position you hold. Yes, you are an administrator for the university. However, your position and success will be defined by your work and accomplishments.

BUILDING A RELATIONSHIP WITH THE PRESIDENT

In some instances, the president of a university or college is practically unknown. You know the president's name and where his office is located. You recognize his name on certain documents. You can pick him out of a crowd at certain events. Understand the president's role as leading the campus on a daily basis. He is most definitely the "big guy" under the big top.

If you serve on a fairly large campus and the university is part of a system, your contact with the president may be limited. Many times, the provost and the other vice presidents will serve as go-betweens for you and others at the university. They work directly with the president. Understand that you will be seen as a member of the administrative team regardless of the number of times you actually work directly with the president.

What might you need to remember regarding the president and working with him or her?

- The president does not walk on water. The position is always more important than the person; however, getting to know the person would be beneficial.
- The president serves as a conduit between the university and the board of regents.
- Never forget your manners or where you are on the university's organizational chart when you are in the president's company. If the president is dedicated to the university and its people, and they usually are, the president will be watching your interactions with others.
- When the president calls on you, regardless of the request, drop what you are doing and take immediate steps to comply with the request—act immediately. Of all the personnel the president has at his or her disposal, the president has called upon you. The request may be in your field of expertise, or the president may feel you can handle the situation. Be sure to let the provost know of the president's request.
- Do the job you were given. When the president meets with the provost and the president asks about the status of a certain situation, you really want the provost to have a response for the president. Your goal is to build credibility not only with the provost but also with the president.
- If the president personally asks you to provide certain information and you do your job and are able to provide the president with the information, do not expect a handwritten note of thanks. Most of the time, you'll get a verbal thank you and that will be sufficient. If the president wrote personal thank-you notes to all those on whom he or she relies, official university business would never get done.
- If you are with the president at an event, formal or informal, the president enters the room first, is greeted first, is seated first, and, usually, is fed first. If someone (a waiter, a colleague, basically, anyone) forgets to follow this protocol or does not recognize the president, you step in quietly, behind the scenes, so to speak, and make sure the president's presence is known.
- If you become aware of some vital information and you feel that communicating it to the president is an urgent matter, but your go-between, the provost, is unavailable for vetting and communicating the information, call the president's office to see if he has time for a very short briefing. If the president is not available, give the information to the president's administrative assistant. As always, be sure to notify the provost of what has taken place and the steps you took.
- Listen when the president speaks, whether in a general meeting or in a smaller setting. You might need to recall some of the information at a later date. Take notes or tape the speech if you need to. Just pay

attention. You may learn a lot about the president and his or her likes, dislikes, and expectations.
- Never, seriously, never say anything bad, discouraging, unpopular, or negative about your institution or its people. If those words ever get to the president's ears, any goodwill you have developed with the president will be lost.

Whoever your president turns out to be and whatever connections you make with him or her, the president deserves to be treated with respect because of the position that he or she holds. Sometimes the person who holds the position may be a little difficult or hard to like. Still, the position of university president should be respected.

EVERY CIRCUS NEEDS A CLOWN

A few people on campus are just a joy to be around. Whether faculty or staff, they are just fun people. When you start getting a little overwhelmed or need a respite from your everyday situations, find these people. These fun-loving clowns will bring a lot of joy into your life when you least expect it. Not only will these people bring a smile to your face, but they will also help you find some fun in the work assigned to you.

The fun people you meet could include a custodian who greets you every morning with a smile. Take a few moments to speak with such employees, find out about their families, when their birthday is, and if they like candy. If such a fun person offers you a friendly gesture, take it. That smile may be the only one you get that day.

As you continue your quest to meet others in the academic community, find a group of faculty in a certain department that is the "fun group." They are there. You just have to find them. These are the faculty that will invite you to lunch, support you in difficult situations, and send you invitations to departmental functions. Be advised that, when you are with these folks, you are not the associate provost. You're just one of the clowns.

Part of your fun might actually stem from one of your responsibilities. Let's try an exercise in having this kind of fun. For the sake of a story, let's say there is a particularly difficult staff member in one of your departments. When he is expected to attend weekend events, somehow he becomes ill or has to take his grandmother to the doctor, again. This person offers negative comments during meetings and takes complaining about office responsibilities to new heights. You have decided to address these issues, in part, by using some of the authority of your position.

Before you schedule a meeting with this faculty member, you send him an email that states the purpose for the meeting and a list of discussion points that will be addressed in the meeting. A few seconds, not minutes, after you hit "send," that person will be knocking at your door asking if there is a problem and what it might be and saying this is the first time he has had any kind of problem in the department.

You might be thinking that this particular situation shouldn't be a time to have some fun, but it really is. Why? Because, in a very respectful way, you are going to handle a situation that has gone on too long. Using a little bit of humor, you are going to make sure this person knows you mean business and are not afraid to address any situation that arises. Bringing in a little humor also reduces your own anxiety about having to deal with a department situation. So, let the fun begin.

- When the person comes to the office with his concerns, set a meeting for a future date. He will be eager to meet with you, but you are extremely busy and will have to meet with him later. This delay might cause this difficult person to be a little more anxious. Oh, well.
- When you do meet with this person, mention the negative comments that he made during meetings and his purpose in making those comments. It wouldn't hurt to have a little grin on your face when talking with this person. The person might offer some kind of an explanation, but just keep grinning.
- Take this opportunity to ask about the continued health of the person's grandmother. The grandmother's illness always seems to fall after hours. Ask if there are other reasons that might prevent the person from helping. Assure this person that, by volunteering to help, he would become a much more valuable asset to the department.
- Take a moment to reflect on the person's responsibilities in the department and ask if he is unhappy in his position. Ask how you can be of help in finding a department on campus where he would be happier.

You may be thinking that the conversation above might not be fun at all. You might be asking why confrontations like this might bring a smile to your face?

- First, the other people in that department are expecting you to take care of them and this person has been a negative force for a while.
- Secondly, your authority as the director of the department needs to be established, and you need to be seen as a leader who is willing to handle any situation that occurs.

- Thirdly, you treated this person with respect and dignity and, if any negativity results from the meeting, it won't come from you.
- Finally, while this might start out as a difficult conversation to have, you should at least have some comic relief by addressing a person who has been known to be difficult and negative. This person will either change some behaviors or look for another position on the campus.

Not all the conversations you have to have as an associate provost will bring smiles to your face. The scenario above should be one that does. The person is a toxic member of the department, and you handled the situation. People have seen you take positive actions to address a departmental need. Not only should you be smiling, but you should also be patting yourself on the back.

This section on finding the clowns and having fun times while in your administrative position cannot go any further without recognizing that, when you have a few thousand students, nay, teenagers, on your campus, there are bound to be a few clowns in the crowd. Some student actions can bring joy and laughter to the entire academic community.

For example, homecoming events are always packed with fun activities. Students paint themselves the school colors. They decorate hallways, cars, trucks, and dorm rooms to show their team support. Some of them get really creative. Try not to be surprised when students come up with unique ways to have fun during homecoming week, even using the campus itself as a backdrop.

Maybe you have a section of the campus where there is a small pond or a reflective pool with a statue of the founder of the university in it. And maybe it's the week of homecoming. One day, as you are walking across campus, you happen to see bubbles, lots and lots of bubbles, coming from that water source. It seems one of those creative students, in his enthusiasm during homecoming week, thought it would be a good idea to put bubbles in the reflective pond, in the school colors, of course.

No matter who, whether faculty members, administrators, or students, walks by that statue, no one can walk by without smiling. No one who sees the bubbles from their office windows will be able to quit laughing. Now, the people who have to clean out the pond don't always laugh out loud, but they will probably grin just a little. Apparently, bubble clowns are just as much fun to work with as other clowns you might meet.

TEACHING YOU HOW TO JUGGLE

Do you know how to juggle? Do you know how to keep plates spinning on top of very skinny dowel rods? If not, start learning. With all of your responsibilities and everything else that is happening around the university, you have to figure out how to juggle your assigned tasks, extra duties, surprise requests, scheduled and unscheduled meetings, and all other duties, as assigned (at least this is what the job description says) and still keep all the balls in the air and prevent the plates from falling. So, let lessons at the School of Juggling commence.

The School of Juggling accepts almost everyone and has a unique set of qualifications for entrance. Anyone applying for admittance must:

- be able to keep track of all appointments,
- master scheduling of meetings,
- write only in pencil because of schedule changes that might take place,
- know what others are thinking and plan accordingly, and
- exhibit a few positive obsessive-compulsive-disorder tendencies.

The ability to leap tall buildings in a single bound is not a requirement but is strongly recommended for each candidate.

If you are already an expert with scheduling and time management, feel free to skip ahead. If not, here are some suggestions that might help you as an associate provost with your plate spinning and ball:

- Keep an up-to-date calendar, either electronically or in writing.
- When planning a meeting, give yourself an unscheduled fifteen minutes before and an unscheduled fifteen minutes afterward. For instance, if you schedule a meeting for 11:00 a.m., on your calendar set the meeting for 10:45 a.m. If the meeting is set to end at 12:00 p.m., on your calendar, the meeting will end at 12:15 p.m.
- If time allows, once or twice a week, don't schedule anything on your calendar until after 9:00 a.m. This gives you a little breathing time before your day really starts.
- Don't keep copies of all the meeting handouts you might get at all of the meetings and university and professional conferences you will be attending. Make yourself some notes. Take pictures of what you want to keep. Find a recycling bin and throw away all the less important handouts.
- Keep a drawer specifically for snacks and bottled water. There are some days when you might not be able to catch a lunch and the snacks will hold you over until you can get a full meal.

- Be sure those in your immediate office have access to your electronic calendar so they may have information about your daily schedule.
- If you choose to use an electronic method to manage your time and organize your meeting schedule, keep in mind phones have to be recharged, internet services could be interrupted, and things do get lost floating around in a cloud.
- Develop a "highlighting" system using a color code to allow you a quick reference to the importance of a meeting. Consider using the same color-coding method you used for your information folders. Red might be the color you use to identify anything related to the provost.
- Give yourself some free time. If time allows and you can have a working lunch with some friends and colleagues, take it and even stay longer than an hour, if possible. It's so good to get away from the office for a while. Just be sure to put the lunch on your calendar.
- Always use the Outlook Calendar (or whichever system you have). Create calendar folders for the directors under your purview so that you may schedule meetings while seeing when these directors are available.
- Get very familiar with Doodle Poll or some similar meeting and event scheduler. Using such a tool simplifies scheduling a meeting with folks in other areas of the university.
- When you know the times, days, and lengths of recurring meetings, put that information in your calendar as soon as you can. This way you won't forget or put something on your calendar for the same time as a recurring meeting.
- There will be times when a person drops by your office and asks if you have a moment to talk. Such a person is really telling you he needs about thirty minutes. If time permits, have the meeting. If your schedule does not permit a thirty-minute meeting, schedule it for another time.

You will develop several other ways to stay on track and to keep your head above water. Your ability to be organized with your time will serve you well. Will every day align with your perfect planning? Probably not. Might you have to make a schedule change more than once in one day? Probably. The point is that, using the suggestions provided, you will be a little more prepared when one of the spinning plates begins to fall.

YOUR PERSONAL WORK AREA

The very first chapter suggested making your office space your very own as part of establishing yourself in your role. Think back to the Hello Kitty decorating tip. Keeping your desk and office organized will also help you with your juggling.

- Benjamin Franklin said, "A place for everything, everything in its place." Live, whether at home, in an office, or in your car, by this motto. Having places for all of your folders, notebooks, and paperwork will save you the time and energy that would otherwise be spent in looking for certain pieces of information. Such organization will be especially valuable if the provost or the president needs that information.
- Your office's appearance is not the point. You may let your office look like a tornado swept through the building, down your hallway, and landed on top of your desk. You may be able to locate every windswept folder. You may even know which stack holds the meeting information you have been looking for. However, at the end of the day, try to have only a few stacks on your desk.
- Consider using a fire-related system: The stack of folders farthest away from the center of your desk concerns situations that are smoldering only a little. The next stack of folders concerns situations that are getting a little scorched around the edges. The stacks of folders closest to your chair concern situations that are on fire and have to be addressed as soon as possible.
- Keep all the supplies you use on a regular basis within reach. This suggestion may sound a little elementary but will save you time. Don't spend time looking for paper clips or copy paper. Find a place for them to live in your office and keep them there.
- As mentioned above, find the best way to organize the many pieces of information that will be coming your way. Color-coding your folders might be helpful. For instance, blue folders could hold information that addresses faculty issues. Green folders cloud could hold information regarding money or budget concerns. You could save the red folder for anything having to do with the provost. Yellow folders could have information regarding student situations.
- Remember one of the qualifications for joining the School of Juggling? You need to possess a few positive attributes of an obsessive-compulsive disorder. You really don't need to touch the door three times before you leave (no humor intended), but having an organized system to address the amount of work coming your way will save you a great deal of time.
- If you are very tech savvy, you may be able to create a system for keeping yourself organized. With this said, electrical devices often "eat" information and need batteries or recharging. Using paper and a pencil to organize your calendar and life as an associate provost still works

fairly well. Just find a system that will keep you on time and where you need to be.

- Always keep any personal belongings put away. You may get to your office at 8:00 a.m. and not step back into the office until after noon. Purses, wallets, and phones that are left on your desktop may be taken. In addition, always keep your office door locked. These suggestions do not imply that ninja thieves are lurking around your office area just waiting for you to leave or that something will happen to your belongings; however, taking precautions is wise.

As mentioned before in a previous chapter, your office space is certainly your own and can be decorated and organized in the way you want. However, whether or not you agree, your office and its atmosphere represent you and, sometimes, your abilities. You will be spending a great deal of time moving in and out of this space. Make it as efficient and comfortable for you as possible.

SUPPORTING THE PROVOST WITH
YOUR JUGGLING ABILITIES

To keep all of those little balls in the air and yourself organized, you have to find a way to stay on time, to arrive at the right meeting, and to meet deadlines. Calendars, whether electronic or paper, are your friends. The secret is using the calendar every time you have a meeting or a deadline.

If you don't enter or write down relevant information (date, time, and place), neither electronic nor paper calendars will be of use to you. You may wish to use an appointment book or a calendar that has a built-in to-do list. Just find some way to effectively and efficiently manage your time.

The first chapter suggested ways in which you may support the provost. The provost relies on you to keep him or her informed, to attend events when he or she cannot, and to be his or her connection with other academics.

Therefore, your time management skills as well as your ability to juggle are essential to your success in your efforts to support the provost.

With that said, how can your time-management skills benefit the provost and show your support for the provost? Here are a few ways:

- If the provost asks you at a meeting whether you have time to chair another meeting on his or her behalf, say, "Of course," and find out the purpose of the meeting and all the details. Don't leave that meeting without this information because gathering this information later will take additional time.

- The time-saving techniques you establish for yourself may make you more available to the provost. It's not about doing more work. It's about building your credibility as a person who can complete the tasks that the provost has assigned.
- Just as you might be pulled in many directions on any given day, so might the provost. If you stay on top of your responsibilities (juggling little red balls and spinning glass plates), you will be able to step in when the provost calls upon you.
- Protect your time through managing it. Protect your days with intentional planning on paper or even on a chalkboard. Whatever system you use, if it is productive for you, stick to it. Then, the system will become second nature to you.

Color-coding and time-management skills will help you when the days become hectic and time is a precious commodity.

With every skill you master, even time management, you show the provost that he or she made the right decision in choosing you to serve as an associate provost. Your efforts to build credibility with the provost must be visible to the provost and others. You may need some time to learn how, at your institution, to complete assigned tasks efficiently and in a timely manner. Be a master of your time and learn quickly.

LET'S LOOK BACK

The circus performers who work under the big top act all together and independently at the same time. They have repeatedly practiced their performances so many times that the jugglers know what's happening in their ring as well as what is happening with the clowns. The circus runs smoothly because positions are known, the performers know their roles, and everyone works with the same goal in mind: to give the best possible performance every day and, thus, to bring happiness and joy to others.

Working in a university's administration, especially as an associate provost means knowing all the players, using time efficiently, and looking for times to have a little fun. Accomplishing these goals may take some time.

Don't forget the importance of using time-management skills to assist you in accomplishing your tasks, in supporting the provost, and in creating a reputation of being on time to meetings, completing projects on time, and being able to assist anyone who calls on you for some kind of help. Learning how to control your time, in your office operations and in your day, is definitely a process. When you take on the role of associate provost, your time management and scheduling abilities need to be on steroids.

It may take you a while to find your way under the big top as you learn the ropes of your new position. Life in administration is a different kind of circus. You have to juggle the responsibilities of your role and the expectations of administration to be successful. One of the most important aspects of time management to remember is to find the way that works best for you, not for others.

LET'S TALK ABOUT THE REAL WORLD

By now, you have a pretty good idea of an associate provost's duties and responsibilities as well as of situations that may come your way when you serve as an associate provost. You have been reminded several times about showing respect to and treating with dignity all who work in the institutional community, regardless of their position. All of these skills are vital to your survival when you work with those in the big top.

The concerns presented in this book are not written to warn you away from applying for the position of associate provost or to encourage you to pack up your office after a month or two. Rather, these concerns are presented to inform and prepare you. Following are some additional simple facts to prepare you for your role.

Your day really doesn't belong to you. Oftentimes, it belongs to the tasks assigned by the provost, to the reports that must be completed, or to the meetings that you have scheduled. Your responsibilities will never diminish and will only grow. Once the provost knows what you can do, you will be called on to be of assistance to the provost. Early in your career as an associate provost, you need to work every day to build your credibility with the provost.

With all of this said, do you feel like you are in the circus, juggling little red balls? Do you think that, with all that will be going on in your work world, you might have to add a sofa, a pillow, and a blanket to your office decor? Do you wish there would be a day when all you have to do is come to your office, put your feet up on your desk, and eat bon bons?

OK, really? In what universe, on what planet, in what dimension do you really think that, as a university administrator, you may have a day to put your feet up on your desk and turn on daytime television while eating a few bon bons? That's never going to happen. If you wanted a cushy type of administrative role at an institution of higher education, you definitely picked the wrong position to apply for.

After attending and organizing a few meetings, after putting in ten- to twelve-hour days, after being at the beck and call of the provost, after a faculty member has called you a couple of unrepeatable names, and after you have seen several students about serious and not-so-serious problems, you certainly have earned a badge of honor and your place under the big top. The good thing is that, if the role of the associate provost doesn't work out for you, you can join the circus as an expert juggler.

The real world in administration is easily described: No two days will ever be the same. If you try to do everything that's on your list without using some kind of organizational system, you will be forever behind. Your responsibilities have require all of your time because the big top (university administration) never closes. The big top, is a business, that business is education, and education is forever changing. Be prepared.

One day under the big top, you might be the guy trying to juggle spinning plates. On another day, you might be the animal trainer fighting off growling angry lions. On any other given day, you might be the clown spreading fun and cheer wherever you go. Regardless of the type of day you have, you have specified responsibilities and the big top needs you.

WHAT WOULD YOU DO?

Following is a scenario to help you with making decisions and choices that will benefit you as you serve in your role as an associate provost. Also provided are some possible steps that you can choose from to deal with or solve a particular situation. After reading the scenario and the possible choices, make some decisions on what you would do. The choices are in no particular order.

The provost has asked you to stand in for a dean at a meeting where a university donor is being honored for her contributions to a department. The agenda for the meeting shows that you will be speaking right after the president. Board members and other community dignitaries as well as many academics from the department will attend. You have spent hours on your speech, making sure numbers and names are correct. Then, the president starts his speech and, as he speaks, you realize that, essentially, he is giving your speech. What should you do now? You are next on the agenda.

A few of these possibilities might be helpful:

___ Listen closely to what the president says. Take some notes on what he doesn't say.

___ Review your speech to see if the president left anything out that you can use.

___ Consider taking some quick notes.

___ Recognize the president, board members, and community dignitaries.

__ Mention the accomplishments of other academics, accomplishments you know of from your work with them.

__ Recognize the dean and the department for their accomplishments.

__ Recognize the donor for her contribution.

__ Mention future goals of the department and how the donation made will benefit those goals.

Chapter 9

Working at the Fair
(Sharing the Workload)

The minute you step on the grounds of the State Fair of Texas, you have entered a working world that depends on people being in the right places, doing the jobs they were hired to do, and making the work behind the scenes look easy. From barkers on the Midway to hamburger flippers in the concession stands, for the duration of the fair, all workers know their jobs and what they are supposed to do. Each one in his or her own role helps to make each year at the fair a successful one.

So, when you head off to buy a corny dog, you are going to witness a well-oiled system in which people know their roles. When you get to the concession stand, someone at the counter will take your order. The worker will turn around to a pan filled with cooked corny dogs, wrap up a dog just for you, and collect the tickets needed to pay for your order. The person at the counter doesn't cook the corny dogs, and the cook doesn't take your order. Workers in the concession stand have defined roles and positions.

Other areas of the fair have similar systems. The person who works at the roller coaster takes the tickets, makes sure the protection bar is locked in place, and pushes the start button for the ride to begin. This worker knows the procedures that are in place for running the roller coaster. While the process for running the Screaming Eagle ride is similar to that for the roller coaster, each of the rides differs in speed, route, and duration. Accordingly, the worker who runs the roller coaster does not run the Screaming Eagle ride. A worker who know the procedures for that ride runs that ride.

Whether working in a concession stand or taking tickets at one of the rides, each worker knows what his or her position is and has a little bit of knowledge about other positions in his or her assigned area. All fair workers work collectively to make their stand or ride have a lucrative fair season. The idea of working together for a common goal isn't new. Whether at the State Fair of Texas or at an institution of higher education, colleagues working together to bring success to the community is essential.

An earlier chapter discussed the concept of "sides of the house." Your side of the house revolves around academics. The other side of the house, the university side, revolves around providing services to students. Some of the best actions you can ever take as an associate provost is to learn who serves on the university side and to develop strong and positive working relationships with these folks.

The worker at the corny dog concession stand is an expert at selling corny dogs, and the ride worker knows how to run the roller coaster. Each one is seen as an expert in his or her field. The staff members who work on the university side of the house are also experts in their respective fields. When these staff members and you as an associate provost connect to help students or to bring success to the university, nothing can stop your efforts.

STAYING IN YOUR LANE

If you are considering applying for the position of associate provost, you probably have several years of education under your belt. More than likely, you have previously served at an institution of higher education and know a great deal about the workings of a university. Additionally, you may have knowledge about how academics departments and colleges operate. This kind of background will serve you well.

However, what if your knowledge about the nonacademic (or university) side of the house is limited? What if you are new to the university? What if you are unfamiliar with university offices, their people, and what they can do to help you help students? These are too many "what ifs," and you have some serious gaps in your knowledge. When the provost assigns you a duty that requires you to work with other university departments, you need to be able to act immediately and work effectively towards a solution.

Quite simply, staying in your lane means you should let experts in their areas do their jobs. There may come a time when you think you can change a degree plan. No, you can't. You might also think you can run your work life without the help of an assistant. That's not even possible.

There will be many things and situations that you can fix in your role. But, when the time comes that you need more assistance in your efforts to assist a student or promote the university, don't hesitate to call on others.

As previously discussed, a university should operate like a well-oiled machine. Such smooth operation is possible only when experts work in supportive roles all over the campus, staying in their lanes, so to speak. You wouldn't want to ask those in the police and traffic department to advise a student on what courses to take, but, when you're securing a parking space for campus visitors, that department should be your go-to.

Some of the offices that are on the nonacademic, university side of the house have previously been mentioned because of their direct involvement with your efforts to address and solve academic, student, and university situations. The staff and personnel in offices on university side exist to be of service to students, academics, and the university as a whole. Calling on these experts to help you is often what you should do. As you continue to work in your position, you should become acquainted with other offices and personnel.

For you, staying in your lane also means you know who to call when you need some specific assistance. You won't call the residence life office to help you with a financial-aid situation. You won't call the food services department to help move a student to another dorm.

Not only do you need to build lasting and positive relationships with the personnel in these departments, but you also need to make sure that their efforts are not forgotten. Unfortunately, because these people don't usually attend academic meetings, they may not be noticed by the academic community. Those who work on the nonacademic, university side are essential to the academic efforts of the institution. One of the unspoken responsibilities of your position be not only to build working relationships with university-side employees but also to ensure that these people are thanked often and properly.

ADMINISTRATIVE ASSISTANTS

A previous chapter mentioned that administrative assistants as special employees who have an unidentified level of power. The position they hold really has no authority; nonetheless, believe me, they possess a tremendous amount of power, especially over your daily life as an associate provost. Whoever serves as your administrative assistant must be credible, friendly, and efficient; he or she will be your right-hand person when you are not available.

Basically, there are two types of administrative assistants. One kind of administrative assistant almost walks on water and has the ability to

- read your mind,
- know exactly what to say to the provost when he or she calls and you are not available,
- keep confidential issues confidential,
- run interference for you and protect your time when a project is due,
- know how to complete timesheets for those who work in departments assigned to you,

- remind you of scheduled meetings and events during your day, and
- bring you lunch when your schedule doesn't allow time for lunch.

On second thought, maybe this type of assistant does possess the skill to do a little foot surfing. These administrative assistants are invaluable, and you should do everything you can to keep these staff members.

Hopefully, you will have this kind of administrative assistant assigned to you. You will most assuredly need this person. With your many responsibilities, your frequent absences from the office, the many university forms that must be completed in a timely manner, and high incidence of situations developing in the departments under your purview, having a dependable and cooperative administrative assistant is a must.

Following are a few questions that you might be asking yourself. (Don't worry. If you don't talk to yourself now, after a while in this position, you probably will.)

- "What if the administrative assistant assigned to me isn't friendly?"
- "What if my administrative assistant doesn't know how to complete the timesheets that are due every two weeks?
- "What if the administrative assistant doesn't play nice with others in other departments?"
- "What if my administrative assistant told a student that he is being investigated for a cheating issue?
- "What do I need to do to let my administrative assistant go? She has been here forever, and I know there will be consequences if she is fired."

The above are just a few thoughts that might be going through your head as you realize the administrative assistant assigned to you has a few shortcomings.

Dealing with an administrative assistant who isn't friendly is easy. Because he takes care of what happens in the office when you can't, arrange some extra time off for him. Because he knows when you don't have time to have lunch and orders you a hamburger, let him take an extra few minutes at lunch. When he asks to go to a doctor's appointment during the workday, because it is the only time he can get an appointment, let him go. This type of administrative assistant won't take advantage of your kindness and, in general, will work even harder for you.

You probably already know where the next conversation is going. You're right. What if your administrative assistant's work falls a little below the high expectations listed above? Being new in your position and trying your best to build relationships in the campus community, what actions can you take that will help your administrative assistant either improve his skills or decide to change offices, actions that will leave you seen in a positive light?

Whether you inherit an administrative assistant or are allowed to hire one, remember the following few things:

- If the administrative assistant has been there for a long period, she or he has some political clout. The administrative assistant may actually belong to the Methuselahs-R-Us Club and may be there long after you have retired. If this is the case, make "nice" early. Learn their birthday, favorite kind of candy, and preferred type of hamburger. Treat them with dignity and respect. Be sure to sit down with them on a regular basis and ask them for opinions and advice on how to handle certain people and situations, provided that you're willing to keep them as your administrative assistant.

- However, what if you do not wish to keep your experienced administrative assistant? Did you remember the fact that this employee holds some political power? Did you forget you're the new kid on the block? In this situation, tread lightly. You might consider giving this administrative assistant more work than they might have had in the past. Set time limits for the completion of these tasks. Double-check their completed work. These actions may seem like passive-aggressive behaviors, and they are. These simple actions may also help Mr. or Ms. Methuselah decide to leave on their own If this administrative assistant chooses to step away from this role, be sure to give them a going-away party that would make the queen of England proud. By doing this, you will honor their many years of contributions to the university and you will have the opportunity to tell others in their circle how much the they t will be missed.

- You may inherit an administrative assistant who is remarkable in the position, who does everything right, who turns in everything on time, and who has only one flaw: he or she is one of the meanest people you have ever met. This administrative assistant may be rude, may be disrespectful to other staff members, and may have the telephone manners of a Nazi general. This administrative assistant might or might not have some political currency. When you mention this employee's name to others, they will say something like, "Oh, you'll get used to her. That's just the way she is."

You can get used to an administrative assistant whose office space is filled with Hello Kitty decorations. You can even get used to an administrative assistant who leaves early on certain days when he doesn't want to fight traffic when leaving the campus. What you shouldn't have to get used to is an administrative assistant's rudeness to you, students, and others. You shouldn't have to redo work that was assigned to the administrative assistant (you don't have that kind of time). You might consider following some of the suggestions below when you're managing an administrative assistant whose work or demeanor is falling short of your expectations.

_____ Start every morning with a "Hello and good morning" directed specifically at the administrative assistant.

_____ Engage the administrative assistant in a positive conversation every morning and every afternoon when he or she leaves for the day.

_____ When planning an office event, ask the administrative assistant what he or she would like to bring, explaining that everyone who is attending the event is bringing something.

_____ If and when you hear the administrative assistant speak rudely to a student, step in immediately.

_____ Make sure your conversations with the administrative assistant are clear and concise.

_____ Create a "script" for the administrative assistant that addresses situations such as how to treat students when they come to the office and how to handle phone calls.

_____ Recognize every accomplishment the administrative assistant achieves.

_____ Review the staff evaluation document with the administrative assistant and provide tasks associated with how the administrative assistant can improve.

_____ Inform the administrative assistant that none of his or her negative behaviors or comments will be overlooked.

A couple of things could happen when you set these parameters in place for an administrative assistant that isn't living up to your expectations. Your focus is on improving the administrative assistant's work habits and helping him or her become the administrative assistant that you need. Understand that, while this might be your focus, it is not necessarily the focus of the administrative assistant. The administrative assistant might feel that you are picking on him or her because he or she never had any concerns until you came. Oh, well.

Whether the administrative assistant recognizes the need to make some changes in his or her professional comments or actions, your need to have an efficiently working office staff has to outweigh the negativity that this administrative assistant's presence could create in the office. An administrative assistant that keeps confidentialities, respects others in the workplace, completes all requests in a timely manner and even before you ask for things to be done, and is friendly and helpful to all students is a keeper. Do your best to value these people every day. They are invaluable.

FIGURING OUT FINANCIAL AID

The financial-aid office does so much to help students. Even though you may not be directly involved with financial aid in your regular duties as an associate provost, some of the student concerns that come your way may involve folks from this office and you need to know who they are. As previously mentioned, the positive relationships you build with this office could actually keep a student in school or provide a pathway for a student to go to college.

You should know the following about the workings of the financial-aid office.

- Students who receive financial aid are required to keep a grade point average of at least a 2.0. If the student's grade point average falls below a 2.0 and the student goes on probation, the student can still receive financial aid for that semester. However, if the student fails to improve his or her grade point average, the student will lose his or her financial aid because he or she did not meet student academic progress requirements.
- Many students who receive financial aid do not know about this requirement. You might be called in to tell students about student academic progress requirements. Most of the time, the financial-aid office will send letters and emails that inform these students that their financial aid will be removed if their grade point average does not improve. This office sends not only letters but also email notifications. Students are fully informed of their financial status. Nonetheless, some students are still teenagers and they have to be reminded to change their socks.
- The intent of financial aid is to assist students in paying for their tuition, housing, and textbooks. In most instances, these funds will be automatically deposited into their university accounts and charges will be debited accordingly. In some cases, a student will actually receive a refund check at the end of the semester.
- You would think that a student could look into the future and realize that his or her refund check would be better used if it were put into a savings account and used for the next semester's tuition and books or dorm bill. Again, recall that some of these students are still teenagers.
- Here is what might actually happen. Students receive their refund checks, immediately spend the money, and then end up back in the financial-aid office worried about how they are going to pay for the next semester. Students don't always understand that, at the end of their college years, they will have to pay back their loans. Very few times will loan forgiveness become a reality for students or their families.
- In most cases, a student has to enroll in twelve or more credit hours to receive full financial-aid benefits. Depending on the student's academic

status, he or she might not have twelve credit hours remaining to complete his or her degree but may need the financial-aid money to complete the credit hours the student does need. In such cases, these students might take extra courses to ensure they can get their financial-aid assistance.

- Unfortunately, some students use this method to have money available to them. Again, they don't always realize that, at the end of their college life, they will have to pay the money back.
- If the provost assigns you to a student situation that involves a financial concern, call your contact person in the financial-aid office and ask him or her to run a report on the money this student has received. This report will give you all the background information regarding the student's financial assistance and will help you make a decision for this particular student.
- Every once in a while, a student will need just a few dollars to stay in school. Again, call your contact person in the financial-aid office and ask if any additional funds might be available. Many employees in the financial-aid office are just as eager to help a student stay in school as you are.

Before you provide any solution to a student regarding financial-aid services, learn exactly what financial-aid monies can be used for. Doing so will save you a great deal of time and effort.. Students often think of the financial-aid office as an open bank for their personal use. This office still has to complete state reports and meet state and federal criteria. These guidelines are ones you need to be aware of when helping students with financial-aid issues.

HELPING HAND OF HOUSING

At most universities, housing (dorm life) is referred to as "residence life." This department handles student housing needs, dorm assignments, and repairs and maintenance of the dormitories. Remember our discussion of the two sides of the house, academic and university? Well, residence life is on the university side. So, why might you, as an employee on the academic side, be called in to address a housing situation?

You may be called in because the president received a phone call about a problem and handed it over to the provost, who then called you. Why you? You know the answer to this one, too. The provost may have called you, because you are a problem solver and you are good at it. Additionally, addressing such issues is a good way for you to show your support for the other side of the house.

So, here's a scenario that might take place. In a previous meeting, the provost mentioned that one of the other vice presidents has a friend whose son will be attending the university in the fall as a freshman. The young man has some emotional needs and would do better if he were in a dorm room by himself. The problem is that all single rooms in the requested dorm are full. It is possible that, with the number of requests the residence life department receives, a parental phone call or request might fall on deaf ears. The parent therefore calls a "friend of the family," the vice president.

You might be thinking that, the vice president, who is on the side of the house that handles this department, could pick up the phone and make the request himself. He could. However, making that phone call might be seen as engaging in favoritism. Such appearances, in some cases, should be avoided. Parents talk to one another. If one parent finds out that a request has been granted because the request came from a personal friend of a vice president, you will not be able to prevent a firestorm from erupting, especially if the denied parent goes viral on social media.

So, you pick up the phone, call the contact you have in the residence life department, and see if something can be done to help the student. By taking on this request, you show the other side of the house that you are willing to help, make certain phone calls, and find a solution. Good job.

You are an expert problem solver now, and the steps below are actions that you might want to consider taking as you solve the situation above

- Inform the provost of the request from the vice president and that you specifically have been asked to help. Don't forget to always keep the provost informed about any tasks you are given by other administrators.
- Learn what you can about the personal and academic needs of the student.
- Ask the vice president who received the request if it would be appropriate for you to contact the parents to let them know you are working on finding a solution. If the vice president says it's OK to call the parents, call them. Let them know someone from the university is working on finding them an answer.
- Contact the residence life department about the situation. Give the department all the information you can, informing the department especially that the request is coming from a vice president. Discuss single-room availability and the possibility of a room change in the requested dorm. Find out when an answer might be coming. There is a specific time when students can change their room assignments. Ask the department to put this student's name on any single room that opens up in the requested dorm.
- Contact the vice president's office and the parents to keep them in the loop.

More than likely an arrangement for a single room can be made; however, the room might not be in the requested dorm. If the requested dorm and the possible new dorm are equivalent in cost and room arrangements, the problem is solved. Not only will you have helped a student find his best new university home, but you will have also added to your credibility and currency with other university administrators.

You need to be aware of another side of this coin. When you ask for assistance from the residence life department or any other university office, you have created a reciprocal relationship. Assure those in the residence life department that, since they were able to help you with a particular situation, they can call on you if ever they need any help. Some staff members in these offices may ask you to intervene in certain situations; be sure to help them when and if you can.

Most of the time, the help such staff members need might come in the form of contacting a parent about a housing issue. Staff members in the residence life department might want you to use a little of your positional authority when dealing with an unpleasant situation or an unhappy parent. Be sure to provide such assistance. Remember that doing so will enhance your credibility and currency and help you maintain positive relationships with others in the university community.

SERVING THOSE IN FOOD SERVICES

Those in the food services department work in two worlds on a daily basis. They are often at the beck and call of administrators who have surprise visitors to the campus and need some refreshments immediately. Because an administrator has made the request, it well be met fully and promptly, perhaps with lemon bars, bottled waters, and cold drinks arriving in a matter of minutes.

This department is also responsible for feeding thousands of students at least three meals per day. For some reason, students and some faculty hold the staff members who work in this area responsible for the foods they serve. In part, they are. However, they are not always responsible for the food ordered, the menu, or why there is no red Jell-O™ that day. Those in the academic community will either love or hate this department and its people.

Again, you might be asking yourself how in the world does the food services department relate to your role as an associate provost. As in working with any other office on the other side of the house, you must follow specific guidelines. You need to be aware of those guidelines when ordering food, preparing for meetings, and adhering to requests made by other administrators.

In your role, you are also trying to build lasting and positive relationships with other offices, including the food services department.

So, following is some information that will help you as you start to develop working relationships with those in the food services department

- There is a specific way to place requests with the food services department. When you begin serving in your role, find out what that process is and live by it.
- Most of the food services departments at universities have a contractual agreement with an outside entity (Aramark, for example). Usually, that contractual agreement states that no outside food should be allowed to be brought on the campus. So, if you are hosting a meeting and need refreshments, you cannot purchase food from Kroger or any such food source. The university's food services department must provide the food.
- The guidelines associated with this office usually require a department or office to order food from the food services department for any meeting that will take place on the campus. You will always be required to give a budget source number to place your order. Before you order any food for any event, make sure you have a budget line. Usually, this budget line amount will come from the provost's budget.
- When you review the ordering guidelines from the food services department, be sure to note the time frames that are mentioned. Usually, orders must be placed two weeks ahead. The time frame will probably also depend on the size of the university and the number of staff members who serve in that department.
- Most food services departments have an online order portal. Locate the order form and complete the information. The information needed usually involves the date, time, place, budget line, person placing the order, and specific food order.
- If you are placing an order for a meeting or event for the provost, be sure the provost has given you the amount you can spend.
- When someone from this office does something special or goes the extra mile to help you, be sure to recognize the person's efforts and let his or her supervisor know. Consider writing a personal note or visiting the director's office in person to share your appreciation.
- Your schedule might not allow you the opportunity to meet and talk with personnel from this department. When you do come in contact with them, do exactly what you have already learned: Introduce yourself by name rather than by title, ask their names, find out a little bit about them (whether they are students, where they are from, etc.) and, as always, treat them with dignity and respect.

Learning as much as you can about how departments work and treating others with respect will redound to your advantage when you need some help. Because you have created some lasting relationships with those in the food services department, they will be more than happy to help you in emergency situations, will forgive you for not adhering to the two-week notification process, and will let you place an order without having a budget line number ready for them. Your being aware of this department's regulations and practices will mean a great deal to the staff members in this area.

PERFECT PLANNING INCLUDES PARKING AND THE POLICE

Two of the most important departments on the campus are sometimes the least remembered when planning for campus events: the parking and police departments. The people in the parking department always have to know when visitors or new employees will be on campus. Examples include ten buses filled with students participating in a University Interscholastic League contest, a chancellor and vice presidents visiting from another university, and new faculty members reporting for work.

In addition, the university police department must be notified ahead of time when something is going to happen on campus. Once again, when the provost puts you in charge of planning meetings, keep the police department staff members in mind. The police department needs to know how many visitors will be on campus, their expected arrival and departure times, and whether they have any special needs (i.e., for special parking places). Their primary concern is the protection of the university and its people.

The men and women who work in the police department are not pretend officers. They can arrest students, issue valid parking tickets, and investigate any situation that comes to their attention. When that parental phone call comes in, you already know what is going to happen. That's right. You will end up trying to find the needed answers and possible solutions. Where do you begin? Some of the suggestions below might be of help to you when solving an issue relating to the university police department.

When a phone call comes from the president, the provost, or another university administrator, asking for your help in addressing a matter involving the university police, consider taking some of the following steps

- Determine what the real problem is,
- Gather as much information as possible about the particular situation,
- Request a meeting with the director of the police department to inform him or her about the current concern,

- Determine the responsibility of the university,
- Inform the provost of your findings (the provost will inform the president), and
- Document your findings.

While the primary concern of the police department is to keep everyone safe, the police department can also help with car issues, including flat tires, keys locked in cars, and dead batteries. Again, if a member of the police department comes to your assistance, mention his or her efforts to his or her supervisors and send a personal thank-you note.

LET'S LOOK BACK

The role of the associate provost, as you can certainly tell by now, is not self-contained. The provost needs to know you can and will handle most of the provost's requests. When the provost makes requests, you will have to know where to go and who to call. You therefore will need to know what departments to call on and who can help you. Time frames should always be considered, and writing thank-you notes after services are rendered is a must. Building relationships with the people in these departments is crucial for your success as someone the provost and others can depend on.

This chapter focuses on individuals and departments whose efforts are oftentimes forgotten. Even when you are just starting out in your new role, do not forget to recognize such efforts. Go back to the university's organizational chart and start filling in the names of the directors of departments, your contact person in these departments, and the names of the staff members that you met along the way.

Knowing these people, appreciating their expertise, and learning how dedicated they are to helping you and the university will help you as you build lasting relationships. The staff members are essential not only to you but also to the students and the community of the university as a whole. Don't forget them and what they do. Recall that you are in the process of building credibility in your role as an associate provost. The respectful way in which you work with and treat the people in the discussed offices will certainly help you.

LET'S TALK ABOUT THE REAL WORLD

From your administrative assistant to the people who park buses on campus, all university employees are part of a system that helps the university run smoothly. Each director of and employee in these departments has his or her own guidelines and protocols. When you have a task that involves such employees, try to help them help you. These offices and their staff members will become essential to your problem-solving.

In the real world, you might have to arrange a meeting in a matter of days, not weeks. In the real world, several events may take place on campus at the same time and on the same day and parking might become a problem. Or, in the real world, the residence life department may not have any room available when you need just one to make a parent happy. On any given day, these scenarios might be on your to-do list.

This and other chapters mention that you should take the time to write personal notes and to visit, in person, to thank directors of departments and their staff members for their extra-mile efforts. Will you really have time to write those notes or visit those offices with all that you have on your plate? It doesn't matter. Make the effort and your reward will be the creation of positive working relationships and help when you need it.

Also, in the real world, the provost is watching the steps you are taking to build helpful relationships. The provost is watching you as you solve the problems that he or she has assigned to you. The president and other administrators are watching how you handle yourself when working with staff members across the university. Building your credibility with folks in offices on the other, nonacademic side of the house helps to solidify your position as an effective associate provost.

WHAT WOULD YOU DO?

You will face real-world situations on a daily and weekly basis. You will have problems to solve, people to contact, and relationships to develop. The scenario below is just one such situation. Provided below in no particular order are some steps that will help you work through the situation and find workable solutions:

After returning from a conference on the rise in the number of college students who identify as homeless, the provost has asked you to develop a plan that will be presented to the president. The provost has informed you she expects your report to be thorough since the president will be presenting it at the next board-of-regents' meeting.

Where do you start? To whom do you talk? What are the university procedures and policies that you have to follow? Here are a few suggestions as you begin completing the provost's request and writing a report for the university:

- __ Because students do not always identify themselves as being homeless for registration purposes, meet with admissions-office staff members to determine if they know of current students who have been identified as being homeless.

- __ Work with the admissions office to add a section to the registration form that allows students to identify themselves as being homeless.
- __ Meet with the director of the residence life department to determine whether a dorm can remain open during the long breaks (spring break, Thanksgiving, Christmas).
- __ Meet with the director of the food services department to determine whether a cafeteria can remain open during the long breaks.
- __ Work with the legal department to determine whether any particular guidelines addresses this issue.

A pause button needs to be pushed right now because of existing university practices.

- Don't be surprised if, when you meet with the directors, you are told that the request is impossible because the dorms, cafeteria, and food courts are all closed during the long breaks.
- Don't be surprised if you are told that hourly staff people are not on duty in the dorms or cafeteria during the long breaks.
- Don't be surprised if finding a solution to this situation takes a little bit more planning.

When you hit this wall, you still might find viable solutions by taking some of the following steps.

- __ Ask the director of the residence life department whether keeping a less-populated dorm open for long breaks would be feasible.
- __ Ask for volunteers from the custodial staff. Maybe there are days they can take to repay lost time.
- __ Work with community members to determine if anyone could help with meals.

The university has several resources at its disposal, resources that can step in to provide a solution for students who identify themselves as being homeless. When you are writing the report for the provost, remember to make suggestions and recommendations only. In this way, the provost can present a viable report to the president. The president will make the final decision, and you will have fulfilled the request from the provost.

Chapter 10

Simple Reminders (Encapsulating What a Day at the Fair Taught Me about Building Positive Relationships)

If and when you get to take a trip to Dallas, Texas, during the last week of September and the first few weeks of October, be sure to visit the State Fair of Texas. You will find some unique food choices, wonderful exhibits, and games and rides that keep you busy and having fun for hours. It's definitely a trip worth taking. The fair has something for everyone, and everyone can find something to enjoy.

While the food, rides, exhibits, and crowds are basically always the same, the fair still offers a few surprises. There are always new cars in the automobile building. There are always baby animals in the petting zoo. And new, experimental fried foods are just waiting to be tried. In addition to the regular mainstay events and exhibits, new things show up every year. Such is the life of a new associate provost. Just as the fair has some constants, you will, too. Meetings, responsibilities, and requests will be your constants. Just as the fair has some surprises, every once in a while, the provost will send you a new assignment or challenge. You'll be ready for any challenge that comes your way.

The previous chapters of this book have given you some insight into the role of the associate provost and the importance of developing and maintaining positive working relationships with those on both sides of the house: academic and university. The topics discussed and the suggestions provided come from lived-and-learned experiences. When you assume the role of an associate provost, you will have your own lived-and-learned experiences.

Each previous chapter had a specific topic and purpose. These chapters focus on how you might learn the ins and outs of the position of associate provost. However, a few things that need to be shared really didn't seem to fit into any of them. Well, Chapter 10 is the overflow chapter. The subjects addressed in Chapter 10 offer more helpful hints and suggestions for you to use as you find your way in your position.

UNDERSTANDING THE MEANING OF MEETINGS

In your previous life, you may have had a meeting here or there. Some meetings might have been regularly scheduled with a definite time limit. Your role at the meeting could have been that of an attendee, the spokesperson, or even a visitor. At your level of academic life, meetings can actually consume your daily and weekly schedule. Here are a few more things to keep in mind about meetings:

- Some meetings are simply perfunctory. These are the meetings that have already been scheduled for the entire semester. For instance, every Tuesday at 1:00 p.m. might be designated as a regular meeting time for you and the provost. Burn this meeting time and day into your memory. This time and date are already on the provost's calendar. If for some reason you have to reschedule the meeting, call the provost's administrative assistant as early as possible.
- When you need to touch base with the provost, be sure to arrange a meeting with the provost's administrative assistant as soon as possible. Tell the assistant the nature of the meeting and how much time you think you will need. The assistant will be able to find you a time to meet.
- Any time you have a meeting with the provost for a specific purpose, be sure to be prepared for that meeting. For instance, if the provost has given you a project and a timeline on an issue with a faculty member, be ready with the information and data you have collected. Do not waste your time or the provost's with just a conversation. Provide the provost with the information he or she needs to make the right decisions for departments, faculty members, and the university.
- Academic meetings are also usually scheduled ahead of time. The provost usually conducts such meetings so that he or she may meet with the deans and directors of the various departments under the academic-affairs umbrella. Attendees are usually the people that you will work with the most. The provost may ask you to speak at such a meeting when new policies may impact academic operations or academic faculty, when a current curriculum issue is in play, or when the provost previously has asked you to report on a particular issue.

- Before such a meeting, stay in touch with the provost's administrative assistant to determine if you are going to be on the agenda for that meeting. If so, be prepared.
- For some meetings, you will have to be prepared to provide information to others, especially deans and faculty members. Be sure to collect as much valuable data and information as you can before the meeting. Avoid giving out incorrect information, and avoid lacking relevant information.
- During some meetings, the provost may hand you a few more new tasks. If so, nod your head in affirmation and add it to your to-do list. You are still in the position and do not have enough currency with the provost just yet to tell the provost you can't handle another task. Additionally, avoid using any kind of negative words, especially the word "no" or the phrase "don't have time for anything new," when speaking with the provost.
- If the provost is at a meeting and needs specific information, be prepared for the provost to call on you for an answer. With your handy-dandy filing system and your knowledge of most situations that the provost has put you in charge of, you will most likely have the answer the provost needs.
- Before volunteering to do additional work, consider what's on your calendar. Think about other reports or tasks that are coming your way. Think about the duties that are associated with the departments under your purview. Remind yourself about what is happening at the university as a whole. Is it the end of the semester when grades are about to be posted? Is a board-of-regents' meeting coming up? While it is very appropriate and necessary for you to offer to take the lead in a matter or to chair a meeting or a committee, your to-do list is still there.
- When you are responsible for arranging a meeting, don't waste people's time. Have an agenda ready. Set a time limit and stick to it. At the beginning of that meeting, tell everyone the purpose and that you understand how valuable their time is and intend to stay on task as much as possible. Also be sure to welcome open conversation.
- Sometimes people attend meetings just to have a vehicle to complain or to give their off-topic opinions. Avoid letting your meeting become such a vehicle by staying focused and in control. Remind the committee member who is complaining or providing irrelevant opinions of the purpose of that particular meeting and offer him or her another time to meet to discuss his or her issue.

Meetings will always be a part of your existence in the world of higher education. Some meetings will be so good that you will leave feeling like you could leap tall buildings, climb Mt. Kilimanjaro, and swim the Nile. However, you will leave other meetings wanting to head home and put your feet up. You may even have a yelling session in your car on the way home. The best advice for approaching meetings is be prepared, be ready, and be in control.

STANDING YOUR GROUND

As a member of the administrative team at a university, you must always stay positive and hopeful about anything that is happening at the institution. Building relationships with those in the academic community is essential to your success in your role as an associate provost. Supporting the provost's initiatives also falls to you as an associate provost. These points have been mentioned and discussed in almost every chapter of this book.

However, at times, you should take care to avoid appearing to be weak or indecisive. At these times, you have to find your voice, make your position known, and stand your ground. Remember how a previous chapter advised you not to be a wuss. Sometimes, you just have to be bold and brave. Following are some of the times that you will need to find your voice:

- If you are present when some faculty members are involved in an angry conversation with each other and the argument they are having involves you in some way, step in and stop the conversation immediately. Remind the faculty members they can be part of a solution but they cannot continue to be part of the problem. Use your voice.
- If you are present when an argument takes place between a faculty member and a dean, step in as the associate provost. End the argument. Offer to meet with each individually. Approach the situation from the point of view that each is an academic and that toxic relationships are destructive to the workings of the university.
- If the provost has asked you to deliver a message and the receivers of the information become angry, stand your ground. Let the angry people vent, let them have their emotions, and remember that the provost appointed you to deliver his or her decision.
- Feel confident in your position wherever you are, whether at a conference or a meeting with various community members,. When you have the opportunity to introduce yourself, say your name, your institution, and your position. Be loud and proud about what you have accomplished—proud but not cocky.
- Let university policies serve as the backing and support you need to be effective and sometimes demonstrative in your role and the

tasks assigned to you. The language and intent of policies can never be overused.

You are an associate provost with a great deal of responsibility. Your staff and faculty members need you to be supportive and knowledgeable. The provost and other university administrators rely on your problem-solving skills to assist them with the functions of the university. Again, you and your position are vital to the workings of the university.

SOME PERKS OF THE POSITION

Here are a few questions for you to answer:

- Are you going to put in countless hours in your role as an associate provost?
- Will you miss family events because you have to attend university functions?
- Will you ever get to the end of your to-do list?
- Will there always be more to do?

You already know the answers to these questions. For all of the times you will be called in to address difficult situations, handle academic issues that arise with faculty or departments, or involve yourself with community functions, your position also holds some perks. An associate provost serves as a member of the university's administration. Because of that status, you will be invited to attend several important university, community, and professional events. When these come your way, accept each invitation and enjoy yourself. You will deserve the perks, which may entail the following:

- Free tickets to sporting events
- Parking passes to various events
- Reserved seating (especially when you are with the provost or president)
- Open access to buffets and other available food offerings
- Free use of university vehicles
- Access to free clothing from various groups across the campus

These are only a few of the perks that are associated with the role you have accepted. The common understanding is that you will not take advantage of any open door offered to you or take too many lemon bars from the buffet table. Perks come from being in the position, not just from being an employee.

While there are several perks to being an associate provost, don't use your position as a pass to cut in line somewhere, to get a special discount from the bookstore, or to get free t-shirts from athletic companies. If the manager of the bookstore gives you an extra discount on a book, accept his kindness. If those in the athletics department offer you a school shirt, take it with much thanks. Don't walk away from a free t-shirt.

THE EVALUATION PROCESS

At the end of every academic school year, you will be evaluated by the provost on your performance during the previous year. The provost should provide you with a copy of the evaluation instrument for your review. You will also have an opportunity to complete a written portion of the instrument that allows you to state your accomplishments, to list the goals you have achieved, and to explain your plans for the next year.

Many of your accomplishments will not be seen directly by the provost. The results of your individual work with students or faculty members might be shared with the provost, but the provost probably is not present to see the actual day-in-day-out work you do. Completing the written response form of the evaluation is your opportunity to share what you have been doing to help the office of academic affairs as well as the university community.

When the time comes for you to complete your written statement, you might want to take a few of the following steps, keeping in mind that the provost doesn't want or need to read a dissertation:

- As an associate provost, keep in a folder, as reminders, all of the programs from special events you've attended.
- Keep your calendar or planner from the previous year as another reminder of the meetings you've been a part of.
- Focus your written statement on academics.
- Add information on how you have helped students, faculty, and community members.
- When you consider your goals for the next year, return to the job description for the position of associate provost. This listing will serve as a starting point. Also, be sure to add any task the provost has given you.
- If the provost has "graded" you below your expectations, you can always ask where you can improve. If you ever receive an evaluation that you think does not really reflect your accomplishments for the year and it's your first year in the position, you have only two choices.

- One, you can accept the evaluation and move on, feeling personally good about what you have been able to do.
- Or, two, you can ask the provost to reconsider his or her evaluation. Please reread choice number one, recalling that the provost is your immediate supervisor and completes your evaluation. Walking on water, ending world hunger, and saving the polar bears do not appear on the evaluation document. Sometimes, you may be the only one who ever knows all the things you do and that has to be enough. Questioning the provost's evaluation of you, especially in your first year of service, might not be in your best interests.

The provost's objective should be to help you grow personally and professionally in your role. You should always try to meet or exceed the provost's expectations of you. Those whom you evaluate should have the goal of meeting or exceeding your expectations. Accomplishments and growth are the keys to a successful evaluation.

You might be asking yourself why this information is in a chapter called "Simple Reminders." This little tidbit reminds you that your accomplishments are for you to know. They are the measures of your duty and commitment to the position and the university.

When you re-examine your appointment book and look inside your folder of collected materials, you will certainly see the contributions you have made. Be gentle with yourself if the evaluation from the provost isn't what you expected.

FINDING BALANCE

If you have achieved this position in higher education, you probably possess the ability to work long hours, eat on the run, and multitask. You might take a briefcase home every evening because the amount of work you have to do is overwhelming. Quite possibly, you cannot turn your brain off to find some kind of rest. If this is not part of your makeup, you are pretty lucky.

As with any position you've previously held, there may not be a supervisor around to see all you accomplish as an associate provost. The provost might hear stories of your abilities to work with others or how you helped another academic solve a pressing situation. Another administrator could tell the provost how instrumental you were in helping an alumni member. From the very first day you step on the campus as an associate provost, you will be busy. Finding a balance will be a necessity for your longevity in the role.

The work, the emails, the responsibilities associated with the various departments under your purview, and all of those colored folders will still be on your desk in the morning when you get there. There will be no little elves that pop out at night to answer all of your emails or solve that student situation you have been working on. They are not coming. Many administrators are able to walk away every day and leave piles of work on their desks. They go home, have some family time, and, possibly, an adult beverage. They find balance.

For workaholics, working at night, working on the weekends, and even working ten-hour days serve as actual therapeutic ways to find balance. If you are one of these type-A personalities, getting things off your to-do list, finishing a report early, or solving a situation in a matter of minutes instead of hours might actually serve as your balance. Don't discount this as being a part of your style of working.

When you accepted the role of associate provost, you also accepted the responsibilities of the position. From this book, you have an idea of some of those expectations. You must also accept that, to do your job well, you need to have some outlets. Join a recreation center on the campus. Take yourself off campus for lunch some days. One day a week, leave a few minutes early. Don't take work home on the weekend.

Learn the best way to live in balance, meeting your job responsibilities and honoring your personal life. This, in some way, depends on the working relationship you build with the provost and the expectations he or she has for you. The university's academic community also will help to define the length of your days. You want to be involved in what's happening since you are new to the role. Let your calendar also help in defining your day. Find balance. It will serve you well.

A FEW PROFESSIONAL REMINDERS

The substance of this section can be written in one sentence: You are always a professional.

As previously mentioned, as an associate provost at an institution of higher education, you always represent the university and the provost's office. Whether you read leadership books, watch videos on how to dress for success, or listen to self-improvement tapes, your actions and words must reflect professionalism. In your various other roles, you probably already know behaviors that are acceptable and things that should and shouldn't be said in public and private settings. The wide use of social media means that nothing is private or personal anymore.

Still, as you learn to move in the administrative circles associated with your role as associate provost, here are some reminders that might be helpful:

- Dress as a professional every day. You never know what is waiting for you on a given day. Will you be working with a student group, meeting with an administrator from another institution, or remaining in your office for most of the day? You also never know when the provost might call on you to attend a meeting in his or her place.
- If this is the case, professional dress may not be required but is expected. Professional dress doesn't always mean wearing a coat and tie or hose and heels. It does mean staying aware of when and where the meeting will be and who will attend. Your position of associate provost should also be reflected in your dress. As archaic as this may sound it is a reality.
- Never cuss or use offensive language to anyone at any time. There may be times when you want to throw up your hands, tell people what you think in not-so-flowery language, or give people a piece of your mind. When you feel that way, stop what you are doing and possibly hum a little song under your breath. Happy Birthday is a good one. Using offensive or rude language is never acceptable for a person in your position. It doesn't matter if everyone around you is using inappropriate language or making offensive comments. You don't.
- Recognize the positions of those in authority positions. Aspects of Leadership 101 remind you that in order to gain respect from others you must give respect. You can show respect by saying "yes, ma'am" or "no, sir" to others. You can show respect by looking a person in the eyes when you are talking to him; doing so is especially important if the person is in a position of authority.
- You always represent the university. If your mascot is a badger, that's right, you are the number-one badger. You have your school colors on. You've mastered that special badger hand signal. You could be at a conference, with other associate provosts, or at a sporting event. Represent the university with pride and, who knows, you may look good in a badger hat.
- Nothing is private, and social media is not always your friend. Let's say you are at a professional conference and you decide to have an adult beverage or, even better, sing karaoke one evening. There is a very real chance that your singing performance might be seen by thousands. Your jaunty little singing career could end up on YouTube.
- Never speak negatively about your institution or anyone at your institution. This has already been mentioned, but this is worth saying one more time. You may work with some of the most hostile people on the planet. The academic community at the university might be struggling to increase program offerings. It just doesn't matter. You work with the most caring and giving faculty. The institution is in the planning stages

of increasing programs in every area and there is no place else you would rather be. You are your institution's best salesperson. Never forget it.

- Whatever supplies are provided at the university, those supplies belong to the university. This includes televisions, cameras, paper, and even paper clips. Anything that has been purchased with university funds belongs to the university.

Sometimes, when there are snacks left over from a meeting, those in the food services department will let you take some leftovers. Do not put these in your car. Do not look at these leftovers as dessert for after your evening meal. Take the leftovers back to your office and share them with the folks in your office. Plenty of university policies govern this one issue.

You may ask yourself, "Why do I have to be a professional when others around me don't have to act right or say the right thing?" or "Why can't I show up on YouTube singing *My Exes Live in Texas*?" You remain a professional, because you are an associate provost and you want to exemplify the reasons for which you were chosen for the position. You also are a walking and talking billboard for your university. Don't let the university down.

Being a professional has many aspects. You may even go to the library or online to continue learning about professionalism. Whatever action you take, being a professional in the role of an associate provost is essential for your tenure in the role.

LET'S LOOK BACK

This chapter provides little reminders for you as you serve in your role. Facing these issues and more will help define your role and actions as an employee at an institution of higher education. You should also realize that these reminders in no way serve as generalizations for the duties you will be assigned or the people that you will interact with on a daily basis.

When you attain your position as an associate provost, you will most definitely make your own way, find your own voice, and be respected by the academic community. In your first year, take your lead from the provost's expectations and do your best to meet and even exceed those expectations. Look for opportunities to find joy and balance in your daily work.

LET'S TALK ABOUT THE REAL WORLD

Here's the thing. There are some days you will want to put on a pair of blue jeans, athletic shoes, and a school shirt. There are some days you will want to have a late breakfast and roll into the parking lot at about 9:00 a.m. And there are some days you look at a faculty member who has just yelled at you and will want to say "Who do you think you are talking to? I am an associate provost and you're not."

The day you decide to take any of these actions will be the day the president is around or the provost is completing your evaluation. Should you be on guard? Should you have to watch every word that you speak? Not really. You just have to be aware and act with professionalism. There are certain reasons for you to speak and act as a professional. Remember, others are always watching, whether at conferences, academic meetings, or on the campus. Colleagues in all areas of the university are waiting to see if they can trust you, if you will live up to your promises, and if you are really a valuable member of the academic community.

There will be days when you want to tell someone to crawl back in the hole he came from and take his petty little problems to someone who cares. This is tough language and also language you will never use. You might think it, but you can never say it. Whenever you feel like these words might come from your mouth, leave your office, take a walk around the campus, or just find a happy place. You are building credibility, positive working relationships, and your reputation as an effective associate provost.

WHAT WOULD YOU DO?

The chapters in this book have focused on your ability to fulfill the role of an associate provost at an institution of higher education. What has been mentioned in each chapter may only scratch the surface of your duties and responsibilities. One thing is for certain: The more you practice addressing different situations that could arise, the better you will hone your skills as a problem solver and a decision maker.

Here is another example of a scenario that might come your way and a few suggested action steps.

They are in no particular order. One of the departments that the provost has assigned to you needs some renewal. The atmosphere is toxic because of the director's attitudes and behaviors. The department morale is so low that the staff members are afraid to be seen talking to you as a member of the university's administrative team. The staff are also at odd among themselves because they feel certain staff members have received preferential treatment. The provost expects you to address each of these situations and help bring positivity back to the department. What are some actions you can take to solve the existing problems?

- __ Meet with the department director to inform her that you will be meeting with ach staff member on a very informal basis just to learn more about the people and what they do for the department.
- __ Before you formally meet with each staff member, find out the way they would feel most comfortable meeting with you. Do they prefer to meet with you off campus or in your office? Which place would make them feel safe enough to talk openly with you?
- __ Take mental notes. Avoid letting the staff members see you writing things down. This might make them feel uncomfortable. As soon as the conversation is over, write down as much as you can remember.
- __ Ask the director for the staff evaluations completed on the people in the department. Review these to see if there are any issues between staff members.
- __ Start being more present in the department.
- __ Begin some team-building exercises with small groups.
- __ Start doing little things to improve department morale. These could be filling up a candy jar and having a raffle for it or buying gift cards to Starbucks and handing one out when you see a staff member going the extra mile.
- __ Conduct a short survey on the climate in the department. Make sure the director of the department knows you will be handing out the climate survey.
- __ Conduct periodic climate surveys. Use the same questions on every survey.
- __ Make it a habit to recognize people in the department every time you can.
- __ Keep the provost informed on what is taking place in the department.
- __ Ask for departmental production numbers before, during, and after you begin your initiatives.

Final Thoughts

If you asked any teacher or administrator I served with what my future goal was, he would tell you that I always wanted to be a professor at the university near us. This was the first of many goals.

I applied to and was accepted into a doctoral program in which, during the next two-and-one-half years, I earned my doctoral degree. I then began my journey into the world of higher education, where I stayed for sixteen years. While living in that world, I never thought one day I would serve a university as an associate provost. No one was more surprised than I was.

One day, my then-current dean came to my office and told me that I should apply for the newly created associate provost position. She thought I would be a potential candidate. So, I applied and went through the interview process. And, lo and behold, I was named to the position.

When I met with the provost and was offered the position, it did not take me long to accept. Of course, that was after my brain remembered to tell my mouth to talk and I wiped the drool from the side of my mouth. Knowing the other candidates, I didn't think I was even a possibility for the position.

As I walked out of the administration building and back to my office, all I could say was, "I am an associate provost. I am an associate provost. I AM AN ASSOCIATE PROVOST." And then, coming to my senses, I said, "How did you become an associate provost?"

As excited as I was to be named to that role, I entered the position with too many personal and professional unknowns.

The stories I have shared here are about the experiences that most affected me and from which I learned the most. I have many more stories about my experiences as an associate provost but wanted to share the most instructive. I have used all of the suggestions listed in this book, and they have worked for me. These suggestions are provided as possible starting points for you when you are given a task and few directions on how to proceed. Some may work for you, and you might add a few of your own.

The purposes of this book are providing future candidates for the position of associate provost with a "heads-up" about the nature of the position and helping those currently serving as associate provosts in meeting their responsibilities. Hopefully, some of the information, suggestions, and reminders in this book will even reenergize currently serving associate provosts who find themselves swamped by their duties.

The book is written as though you, the reader, and I are sitting in a cozy restaurant, having a cup of coffee and a piece of apple pie. Throughout the book, I have had little conversations with you to prompt your thinking and to help you reflect on what best practices might be. The "Points to Ponder" and "Note to Self" sections are included for this purpose.

I hope that reading my stories will, in some way, help you in your service as a valued and successful associate provost and member of your academic community. If and when you are made an associate provost, you will write your own stories, address your own situations, work with your own people, and make your own decisions. Perhaps knowing about my lived experiences, from reading this book, might be beneficial as you make your way through the learning years.

Remember to find some joy in what you do and the people you work with. Learn to take some time for yourself. Accept your accomplishments with grace and be a servant to all.

Best of everything,

JT

Made in the USA
Las Vegas, NV
27 January 2024

84978206R00100